Papa Cado

M.G. CRISCI

A True Story

Orca Publishing Company   San Diego   2017

Designed by Good World Media
Edited by Holly Scudero
Cover Art: Papa Cado Portrait by M.G. CRISCI

Manufactured in the United States of America

Library of Congress Control No.
2009907911

ISBN 97809663360-2-3
Enlarged Fifth Edition

Also by M.G. Crisci

ACE 44
Call Sign, White Lily
Indiscretion
Mary Jackson Peale
Now & Then
Papa Cado's Book of Wisdom
Salad Oil King
Save the Last Dance
Seven Days in Russia
This Little Piggy

Learn more at
mgcrisci.com
ace44movie.com
twitter.com/worldofmgcrisci
YouTube.com/worldofmgcrisci
Facebook.com/worldofmgcrisci

To Arthur,
My hero, my role model, my brother

Table of Contents

Peaks and Valleys

Letters from Arthur

Letters to Arthur

Preface

I MET ARTHUR MERCADO, known to his four granddaughters as Papa Cado, some time ago, at the Scripps Hospital Healing Hearts Program in Southern California, where we both live.

Why was I there? My high-powered, self-consuming business career had left me little time for a balanced lifestyle. In other words, I had allowed myself to become a genuine candidate for a heart attack. Two years prior, I had been diagnosed with a cardiac condition called atrial fibrillation—a fancy medical term for a racing heart. While my doctor reassured me, "We don't have any actual research on the correlation between life expectancy and atrial fib, so you'll probably live a *relatively* normal life. However, there was a caveat, "But, you realize you are now in a different risk category."

She also "suggested" I enroll the hospital's heart healthy program, which she described as "an innovative, holistic approach to lifestyle change." It only took me 24 months to heed her suggestion! By then, I was sick and tired of taking pills that made me lethargic and light-headed. I visited the program director. She took one look at my pouch, gave me the 60-second overview, took my credit card, smiled, and welcomed me. "We think you'll find the 12-week program quite comprehensive." The program curriculum included classes in Yoga, Spirituality,

Stress Management, Nutrition, and Vegetarian Cooking. I was rather skeptical, to say the least.

Day 1 found me in the gym with four overweight, middle-aged men and women grunting and groaning. Day 2 was filled with stress-management support sessions—a first for me. Next thing I know, I'm sitting in a semi-circle. This gentle, soothing sounding dude named Ozzie introduced himself as "the group's facilitator." He asked us to hold hands. It seemed a little effeminate to a preconditioned-macho man like myself, but I'd already spent the $2,800 bucks, so I put my hand out. Somebody else touched it. I looked straight ahead.

Ozzie asked how we felt. You could hear a pin drop. Since I was an accomplished public speaker, I volunteered to go first. I figured my new "best friends" might as well hear my tale of woe, so they understand how lucky they are not to have my problems.

I spoke about five minutes. Ozzie nodded. Kris, Keith, Shirley, and Arthur said nothing. After all, nobody was allowed to place value judgments—it was part of the ground rules. I thought to myself, 'good on ya.' Probably shocked the hell out of them.

They each began to recant their stories. For some strange reason, I decided to listen. (I've never been considered a great listener by anybody).

Twenty minutes later, I concluded I might be the luckiest man in the world. Kris told an incredible story about the loss of a limb he had dealt with since birth. Shirley has endured enough pain and suffering to drive you to atheism. And Keith, who appeared healthy as a horse and strong as a bull to boot, was looking for someone to explain why he was filled with rage.

The final member of the support group was a gray-haired man wearing gray pants, white t-shirt, white sneakers and a thick gray beard and glasses, sitting to my right. He hadn't moved a muscle or uttered a word. I said, "And, what about you?" He stared blankly and scowled deeply. 20 seconds of dead silence seemed like 20 minutes. Then he spoke. "I'm Arthur. I told *those people* that I don't like to talk about myself."

Even though I'm loathed to make value judgments (joke), I concluded he was borderline manic depressive or a deeply introverted personality on a quest *not* to identify.

I was also happy I was not within *swiping range* of the switch blade he surely carried in his back pocket to open beer cans and slice mangoes.

I also decided I was going to make it my job to crack this guy's shell. After all, I had *the* secret weapon—my bizarre sense of humor. (I find myself hysterically insightful, all the time).

"So, Arthur, is that all there is to that?"

He stared at me. I tried to smile. Frankly, I was a little intimidated.

"The doctors tell me I have no right to be here," he revealed calmly. "I'm sixty-three, and I've beat death twice. I love my wife (his third) and my only daughter, who I raised by myself, and my four wonderful grandchildren. I'm just doing the best I can to avoid dying right now." He paused. "And, that's my story. Satisfied?"

My arrogance melted to insignificance.

His hand began to shake. "Damn hand, never used to do that. It's that Parkinson's thing. But the good news is when it shakes I know I'm still here!"

He smiled. We all laughed. He touched the heart of everyone in that room.

Over the next twelve weeks, I learned there was much more to Arthur's story than just the 28 stents, 11 angioplasties, a five bypass, multiple mini-strokes, nitro patches, and numerous other cardiac procedures. I decided people needed to know Arthur. And, so it was that he agreed to sit day after day and reveal his hopes, dreams, wishes, and life in what I call *Arthur speak*. In the process, I learned we all have much to learn from him. I am honored that this kind, gentle man agreed to share his extraordinary journey through life.

I'm confident you will be inspired by Arthur's simple yet elegant approach to living a dignified life. I only hope I did justice to his insights, his wisdom, and legacy.

Part One

Growing Up

Chapter 1

The Wall

*This is me at age 3 (little guy on the left) with big sister Lori and brother
James. Notice my fancy duds.*

I WAS BORN AT A YOUNG AGE....on September
8, 1944.

Like most kids that age, I don't remember much.

We lived in a modest but clean apartment complex in
Mobile, Alabama, while Pop was stationed in the Coast
Guard. Pop was a lot of things, including proud,
generous, hard-working, and tough as nails.

He believed nobody should push you around. But
there was one thing he was not. He was not affectionate.
In my entire life, he only hugged me once when I was 18
years old. But more about that later.

Anyway, my first real vivid memory of anything was
that Sunday. Typically, Sunday was Pop's day of rest—he
worked six long days a week in the Coast Guard. He

made it a point to spend most of his free time with the family. This particular Sunday, Mom, and Pop took me, James, and Lori to the park a few blocks from our apartment. They had decided a picnic was in order. As you can probably imagine, my recollection of the precise details is a bit hazy, although sixty years later, some things remain crystal clear.

I was wearing a light-blue outfit with short pants, just like in the picture. We walked past a white cinder-block wall about three feet high. I looked up. To me that wall was so high, it almost touched the sky. Pop looked at me staring, and smiled. He was about to teach me my first lesson of life. I guess he knew from some earlier experience—I don't remember why or when—that I was afraid of heights.

Pop whispered something in Mom's ear. I remember she started pleading, "Arthur, please don't." Pop's full name was Arthur Gallo Mercado. He was Mexican. Mom was a purebred Caucasian named Ernestine Lily Mae, whose mother freaked out when she discovered her daughter had married a Mexican.

Mom's pleading didn't do much good. Pop was a man on a mission. Next thing I know I'm standing on the wall, and he's walking away. I began crying like a frightened three-year-old. Surprise! He started spreading a picnic cloth on the ground like nothing happened. I think Mom was afraid to say anything else although I'm not sure about that—I was too busy bawling at the top of my lungs.

"Arthur, come on down," said Pop calmly. "Time for lunch. Mama's made some tasty sandwiches."

I looked at the rocky ground as the tears streamed out of my eyes. It appeared to be light years away. My knees wobbled. I became even more frightened. My hands began to shake uncontrollably. I desperately wanted to get down, but I was frozen in place.

Mercifully, after what seemed like hours, Pop finally took notice. Some time later, Mom told me Pop had left me standing there for only 30 seconds. I honestly don't think Pop fully comprehended how prodigiously steep a four-foot wall looked to a three-year-old kid. He walked over, stared in my eyes—I'll never forget his disappointed expression—and said, "La Voughn (I didn't become Arthur until the third grade), do you need help to get down?"

I nodded yes. "Pop, take me down, take me down." I extended my hands. Pop held them firmly as he removed me from the wall.

Once on the ground, I started apologizing. I knew. "Pop, I'm so sorry." My hands and body continued to quiver.

He knew I was embarrassed. But he refused to hold me in his arms or console me.

"Let's eat. I'm starved. La Voughn, want a sandwich?"

The fear subsided. My hand stopped shaking.

"La Voughn," he explained, as we sat on that picnic blanket, "let me tell you something. *It's okay to be afraid. Just don't ever let it stop you from doing what you need to do.*"

That's the way I lived my life the next 60 years. And plan to live whatever time I have left the same way.

Chapter 2

Toasted Pecans

Mom and Pop in Mobile Bay.
We had a real house, a backyard, and a big pecan tree.

LIFE WAS GOOD.

When I was five, we moved into a small house off Mobile Bay. I think the name of the street was Dearborn.

We lived across the bay from the shrimp boats. Some Saturdays, when Pop got off duty, and we had a little extra money in the family jar, we would drive over to the boats and buy some of the day's catch. Then we'd come home, and Mom would make one of Pop's favorite dishes in the whole world, shrimp gumbo.

Our house had a white front porch and a small back yard, which was quite a change from our little apartment. Smack dab in the middle of the back yard was the largest pecan tree in the world! My world, that was. By late summer and early fall, the tree was full of pecans. By late fall, the leaves and pecans started to tumble down in significant numbers. Mom used to say, "Gallo, make sure you clean those leaves; don't want the children to slip and fall." Pop would take the rake, make a big pile, pecans and all, and burn the stuff until there was nothing but embers.

One day, James said to me, "Something sure smells good in that pile."

He figured it was the pecans. So James went into the nearby woods and came back with a long branch that had a fork-shaped end. He went over to the smoldering embers and carefully pulled a few pecans from the pile. "I'm guessin' the dark ones are cooked," he said.

I reached over to pick up one. My scorched finger told me the shells were hot as hell! We waited a few minutes until they were hand-friendly. James bounced one on the cement walk to crack the shell. I did likewise. Moments later, we were eating the yummiest, sweetest pecans ever.

Pop walked over with a scowl on his face. "You boys messing up my work?"

The cat got James' tongue.

I handed Pop a toasted pecan. He smelled it, and started to eat it. Then he did something out of the ordinary. He smiled. "You boys making something out of nothing. Good thing to know."

I've been *making lemonade out of life's lemons for a long, long time.* People that know me tell me I'm resilient as hell. I just wish sometimes I didn't have to harvest so many lemons.

Chapter 3

Castleberry Christmas

Me age six,
at Grandma's annual family Christmas celebration.

CHRISTMAS EVE AT GRANDMA'S was always a wonderful time, full of rituals and good cheer. Plus, Grandma seemed to have a knack for the dramatic.

The Christmas tree always stood in the corner of the living room, steps from the fireplace. By the time the family gathered, Grandma—"Ali B," as my sister Lori called her—had decorated the freshly-cut tree with ornaments, some made, some purchased. There was an empty stocking for each of the kids sitting under the tree.

Grandma would bring out a rope line and tie it from the window by the fireplace across the room to the door by the kitchen. She'd always got Pop to help. The adults would drape quilts over the line, enclosing the fireplace and the Christmas tree. The *hide and seek* ritual made the excitement of Christmas morning unbearable.

Next, Grandma would announce, "Time for some apple cake." We would march into the kitchen, where the most scrumptious whiskey-soaked apple cake sat on the table. From the point of view of a six-year-old, the stuff was fabulous. To this day, I can still smell and taste the whiskey in that cake. I also remember thinking, *How adult! Sucking down whiskey just like Mom and Pop.* The entire family ate, told stories, and had a jolly time in the kitchen.

This one particular Christmas, we heard the sound of footsteps on the roof, then some scuffling in the living room. "What is that racket?" asked Pop.

"I didn't hear anything," smiled Grandma.

"Well, I'm going to check it out," persisted Pop.

"Not just yet," responded Grandma.

There was dead silence.

"Now," said Grandma.

We all returned to the living room and watched Grandma remove the quilts from around the Christmas tree. I was the first to notice a change. "Look, Grandma, the stockings are filled." They were filled with fruits, nuts, and a huge peppermint stick.

Lori noticed the packages wrapped in different colored paper next to the tree.

James walked over to the fireplace. "Look at this," he said, pointing to soot footprints that went from the fireplace to the tree and back.

That evening, at the dinner table, we asked Pop and Mom how Grandma did the Santa Claus trick, since we were all present and accounted for. "I don't know," said Pop. "Honest."

We turned to Grandma, who had just entered the room. She had a big smile on her face like she knew something. We begged and pleaded to identify "the who." She just shook her head. During the next four Christmas Eves, the same thing happened. Even Pop and Mom began to wonder how she did it.

Eventually, we moved from Castleberry, and Grandma passed.

She died without ever telling anyone what actually happened. To this day, I wonder if Santa really visited grandma's house. I know what you're thinking: Santa is a fabulous myth passed on through the generations. But, just suppose...

Now and then, I remember Christmas in Castleberry, and I ask myself, *because you can't reach out and touch something, does that mean it doesn't exist?*

Chapter 4

Tough Times

*Me (front, right), James (rear), and our friend Bunky,
not long before we moved to Grandma's.*

MOVING INTO GRANDMA'S house was a treat
and a disappointment. I'm now age seven. Unbeknownst
to me at the time, after the Coast Guard, life got hard for
Pop. He wasn't making much money selling Bibles door-
to-door. So he got a job at nearby Shelly Air Force Base
in civil service, whatever that was.

I surmised Pop's pay was low since before long he
was looking for another job. But, there didn't appear to
be much application for his Coast Guard skills in the
local economy, so he and Mom decided to move to
greener pastures in California—at least once they had
saved enough to have a roof over our head while Pop
looked for work.

Moving was more traumatic for James and me. We
had made a lot of friends in school and didn't want to
leave them. Bunky was our super-best-friend in the whole
world. The three of us played baseball every chance we
got. The day we left for good, Bunky gave James and me

a brand-new baseball he had just gotten from his father. I can still see the tears in Bunky's eyes as we drove away. For some reason, I didn't cry. It didn't seem right. Bunky was sad enough for the three of us.

I'm not sure whether Mom's mother, Grandma Alibi, volunteered, or Dad just flat out asked. All I remember is we were driving under the Tallulah Bankhead Tunnel on the way to Castleberry, Alabama. Dad turned around, in his usual stern tone and manner announced, "We're going to live with Grandma Alibi for a while, so be good."

Grandma's place was a big old, sprawling house with more bedrooms than she could ever use. The back yard seemed huge compared to our postage-stamp yard in Mobile Bay. Of course, Grandma was not exactly Jake Gatsby. The house had no gas, no electricity, and no running water But, no matter, the back shelf of the wood stove in the kitchen always had a pot of her Louisiana specialty, red-eyed gravy and a plate of homemade biscuits there for the taking. They were absolutely deeelicious! I can still smell the aroma and taste the crumbs as they slid out of my mouth and down my overalls.

The sink had a hand pump. Grandma used to keep a pitcher of water by the sink to prime it. That was always my job. Making sure we always had water when needed taught me responsibility

We had two ways of taking a shower. You could go out in the back and pull a cord on a bucket. Man, was that water cold! When Pop could afford it, we went to the barbershop in town, where for five cents a person, we could take a hot shower. That was *almost* as nice as Grandma's biscuits.

~

The back yard rewmined me of a swamp. No...It was a swamp. We had alligators, copperheads, water moccasins, and a bunch of other animals I don't remember. It was great! One day, a deer had the misfortune of wandering into the yard. Grandma took out a rifle which was almost as big as her, placed it on her hip, and shot the deer flat out. We had venison steak for the next week. Every night was like a special Sunday dinner.

The best part of Grandma's house was the bedroom where James and I slept. There was a small fireplace in the corner to stay warm on even the coldest days. But the pièce de résistance was the featherbed. When you laid down, you were enveloped in six inches of the softest, most comfortable feathers. It was like sleeping on a cloud. When we pulled that thick comforter over us, all seemed right with the world.

Grandma taught me a lot during that year. *I learned there are no free rides in life; everybody has responsibilities. Most of all I learned that being loved unconditionally is the greatest feeling in the world.*

~

I don't remember exactly how long we lived with Grandma in Castleberry, maybe a year or two. But eventually, the time came. Dad and Mom packed our 1949 Chevy, and we headed to Los Angeles, California, right after Christmas.

Best I can remember, the year we moved I spent the third grade in three different schools. The first semester in Mobile, the second in public school in Los Angeles, and finally a little Catholic school in L.A. It was there I officially became Arthur.

Chapter 5

James Mischief

&

Arthur Angel

*Brother James (left) and myself
during one of our infrequent well-mannered moments.*

I WAS THE PERFECT ANGEL growing up. Never got into trouble!

As I recall, older brother James was the family's head mischief-maker, even though he was considered the "quiet one."

One of James's favorite things was to tease our sister Lori. Nothing big, just dropping bugs in her doll house, hiding her favorite toys and stuff. It pissed her off, but she took the blows, except for this one time when they had a raging argument Lori picked up a butcher knife and started waving it, while James decided to defend himself with Mom's broom handle. You should have seen the expression on Mom's face when she came into the kitchen to find out what all the commotion was about!

~

Jame's next favorite thing was for him and his friends to tie me to things—like chain link fences—and just leave me dangling. I still remember one of the most embarrassing times. One day after school, James and his buddies hogtied me to a big tree near a porch in some yard down the block. When the lady came home, it was nearly dark. She was horrified and wanted to call the police. I just said, "I'm okay ma'am, it was just my brother and his friends. They do it all the time. But, I would appreciate if you'd untie me. Pop gets real mad if I'm late for dinner."

~

Most of these little pranks tended to happen when Pop was at work. Mom, who was cute as a button and all of 102 pounds soaking wet, was the de facto family daytime disciplanarian.

If there was one thing I learned early on, you didn't give Mom any crap. But for some reason, James never got the message, until this one particular day.

Mom was watering the flowers with a garden hose. James and I were sitting on the front porch reading comic books. James decided to tease Mom. I don't know why. He walked over to her and whispered something. I never found out what.

Next thing I know, Mom was furious. She doused James with water and started yelling at him. He ran, she chased him. She was so mad; she forgot she had the hose in her hand. The next thing I know, the fully extended hose went straight up into the air with Mom's hanging on for dearlife. She finally had to let go, and landed on her rump. The whole scene was hysterical. I can still remember me smiling from ear-to-ear on the porch.

Mom glared at me. I hightailed it to the back porch. I must have sat there for more than an hour in fear that Mom would come after me. I heard some rustling. Then James began to wail on the other side of the house. I remained paralyzed.

That night at the dinner table, nobody said nothing to anybody about anything.

~

Despite being Arthur Angel, I managed to get into a fair number of fights growing up. I'm proud to say I usually beat the crap out of the other guy because I *never underestimated the power of my opponent, no matter how small he appeared.*

Despite James's quirkiness, he was a loyal brother who understood one of his "big brother" responsibilities was to make sure no harm came to me.

One day on the way home from school, we had to walk by the house of the school's baddest bully. I knew James was intimidated by him. We walked across the street to avoid passing directly in front of the house. The kid came out the door and started calling me names like wimp, sissy, etc. Finally, James had enough. He walked over to the bully, who was about six inches taller and maybe 30 pounds heavier—quite a discrepancy at the age of 14.

James said, "I'd stop with the names. Not right."

The bully glared and responded, "Says who?"

Next thing I know, James hauled off and hit the bully so hard, he dropped to the deck. And, that was only the beginning. As the bully struggled to his feet, James pounded the guy into oblivion. The bully bounced off garbage pails, the wall, and finally the hood of a car in the driveway.

As James and I walked home, neither of us said much. But I was proud of my brother. He had taken Pop's philosophy to heart—*it's okay for family to fight, but when somebody challenges the family it's time to close ranks.* The funny thing was, when we were full grown, James was about 155 pounds, while I was a buff 230 pounds with a 32-inch waist. But he was always my "big brother," and Mom always intimidated the hell out of me.

Chapter 6

Cracker Jacks

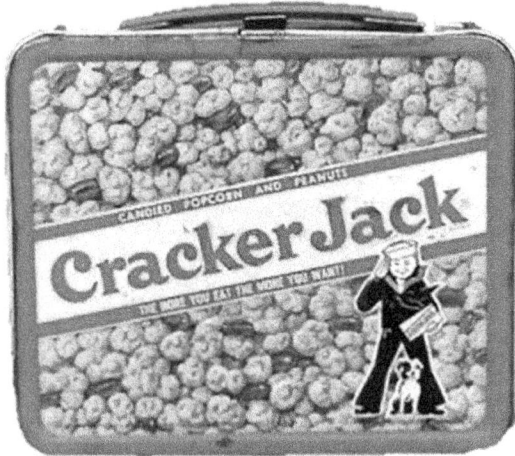

I loved the little prize in every box. So did Pop.

IMAGINE A GROWN MAN TRYING to beat a couple of kids out of their Cracker Jack prizes?

It happened in our house with some regularity. Pop would come home from work with three boxes of Cracker Jacks. After dinner, James, Pop, and I would sit on the living room floor, find the prizes, and nibble on a few kernels of caramel corn and nuts. Somewhere in the middle of nibbling, matters always turned to trading.

Pop wanted to wind up with the neatest prizes, based on whatever was in vogue at the moment. Once they were in his possession, he would point out we had been outsmarted…again. Pop knew we knew the whole ritual was just a big game, but James and I always let Pop have his because the entire negotiation ritual was great fun. In some ways, this tough man with the big heart was like a little kid.

~

As I recall, one evening, James and I had concluded the coolest new Cracker Jack toys were the miniature magnifying glass (because it could fry ants on a sunny day) and plastic whistles (because you could hide behind cars and make people wonder where the policeman was).

James opened his box first. Sure enough, there was a magnifying glass. Pop made a big deal out of the fact that it was too small to read anything. He offered James his blue plastic buffalo. "There are lots more animals so you can create a real farm."

"Pop, I'd like to keep the glass."

"James, you sure?" It was now clear Pop had locked and loaded on the magnifying glass. Pop upped his offer. "How about a buffalo and a squirrel for the magnifying glass? It's a really great deal. Two for one." James accepted. Both of 'em won!

It was now my turn.

"Arthur, check your box," urged Pop.

I had tattoos. "Look Pop, tattoos I said excitedly. I'll put them on my hand and where them to school." Next thing I know I had traded Pop my tattoos for a plastic poodle. Ugh!

Once Pop had the tattoo strip in his hand, he transferred two images to his hand. "You boys should be aware," he crowed, "You gave away the best prizes. Here, look at *my* tattoo through *my* magnifying glass."

We were ready to cry. Pop noticed. "Got some extras he said." Pop took the remaining tattoos and put on on Jame's hand, the other on mine. We looked like Indian warriors. The three of us started chanting a war dance around the house. Mom wasn't sure who was the father and who were the kids.

~

Our post-trading celebration was always the same. Pop would officially declare himself the best trader. Then he'd take us down to the Thrifty Drug Store and buy a big five-cent ice cream cone for each of us. The whole ritual was kind of silly, but it taught me that *a grown man should never lose his sense of humor. Laughter makes everything right with the world.*

Years later, in the real world, I sold insurance, then luxury cars. I was a top producer in both areas. My associates always thought I was a "natural-born" salesperson with an uncanny ability to close prospects. Never told any of them that I became a good salesman because Pop gave me an advanced course in horse-trading with Cracker Jack prizes.

~

Pop was unpredictably consistent. He'd do anything for a laugh.

It was Christmas Eve, a few years after we stopped trading Cracker Jack prizes. By now, I'm a buff, strapping teenager. I'm thinking cars and imagining participating in the Junior Mr. America competition. Pop had recognized my new passion earlier in the year and bought me a set of barbells.

As was the tradition in our house, Pop handed out the presents to the kids. First Lori, then James, and then myself. Being last always heightened my sense of anticipation.

Pop picked up a box from under the tree. The present was of reasonable size with the prettiest gold wrapping paper and a big red bow. I couldn't wait to rip it open.

"Merry Christmas."

He practically flipped the box into my hands. I reached out to grab it. To my surprise, the box must have weighed a hundred plus pounds. Damn near gave me a double hernia. I fell to the floor.

"Aren't you gonna open your present?" smiled Pop.

The box contained a serious collection of additional weights for my barbells. I looked up to say thanks because it was a super cool gift. But I couldn't get a word in edgewise; Pop was laughing too hard.

Chapter 7

Mom's Favorite Son

Mom liked Lori. Mom liked James. Mom liked me.
But, Mom loved Peppi.

LIFE WASN'T THE SAME AFTER that visit to the pet store.

James and I were looking at the dogs playing in the fenced area located in the front of the store. Pop smiled. I sensed he thought the house could use a pet. Mom thought the same thing. Her eyes wandered past a tank full of colored fish and cages of parrots and cockatoos.

She spotted this cage in the rear of the shop that housed a white-faced capuchin monkey. The shopkeeper said, "Careful ma'am, Peppi is a little wild."

"Where's he from?" asked Mom.

"The forests of Costa Rica. Very intelligent. Just very high strung."

I walked near the cage. He demonstrated his fangs. I got his point…keep your distance. He began waving his long tail and arms. Mom walked closer. "Hello, Peppi."

The damn thing calmed down immediately, turned his head, and looked wistfully at Mom.

"What does he eat?" she asked.

"Pretty much anything. He's not fussy."

She picked up a piece of fruit lying outside the cage and reached out to Peppi. He gently removed the fruit from Mom's hand, shook his head as if to say thank you. It was scary. She melted.

For the next few weeks, whenever we passed the pet store, Mom would walk in and ask if she could feed the monkey. As soon as the damn thing saw Mom, Peppi would calm down and walk over to her. Then he'd lay in her lap while she fed him. As soon as we left, you could hear the monkey begin screeching.

One day, the angry owner said, "This is the last time you will get to feed this crazy animal. Anytime somebody shows an interest in him, he screams and bites. Next week, Peppi will be no more."

A horrified Mom walked over to Pop. They talked quietly. He nodded. "Mr. Johnson," my Mom said sweetly, "we'd like to buy Peppi, but the price on the sign is far more than we can afford."

The owner knew Mom wanted the monkey, and he desperately wanted to get rid of Peppi. He made an offer. Pop accepted immediately. No haggling. That's how I knew Peppi was a good deal.

Mom walked over to James and me. "How would you boys like a little brother?" We were actually kind of excited about being the only kids in the neighborhood with a pet monkey...even though we knew, he could bite the hell out of you if you weren't careful.

~

We took Peppi home. Mom and Pop set up a cage in the garage. It was about four-by-four and sat on two sawhorses just high enough for our dog to walk under it. I think Peppi hated other animals more than boys and men. During the day, when Mom was home, she gave the damn thing free run of the house, but at night, we'd put

Peppi in his cage and shut the light out by covering him with a blanket.

One night, we're watching TV after Peppi had been put to bed. There was this horrible screaming coming from the garage. We ran as fast as we could. There was our poor dog with his ass in the air and the monkey yanking and biting his tail. The dog learned it's lesson. It never again walked close to Peppi's cage, covered or uncovered!

~

Things went from *good to bad* in the Mercado household. Peppi unofficially became number-one-son. For goodness sakes, Mom even spoiled the thing with fresh grapes. Peppi would sit and peel the skin. Then he and Mom would sit side by side and laugh. It was eerie having a monkey for a brother!

It seemed Peppi could do no wrong while we got blamed for everything. Mom used to make coconut cakes, then cover them, and tell us not to sneak a snack. "Boys, keep your hands out of there," she'd warn. "That's tonight's dessert." Like obedient sons—at least some of the time—we'd stay clear of the cake. But not Peppi. After she left, he'd raise the cake cover and help himself to a nible or two from the bottom of the cake. When Mom returned, she'd be ready to scold us. We'd tell her what happened—out of self-defense—then she'd just laugh, "Isn't that cute!"

~

Before long, things went from *bad to worse* in the Mercado household. One evening, Mom and Pop gave James and I the rare privilege of eating TV's dinner on trays in the den. We didn't notice Peppi had entered the room. Suddenly, two little black hands grabbed our biscuits and ran down the hall yelling. Mom reprimanded us for letting Peppi have our biscuits because "it was not the proper food for a monkey."

Another time, Mom had rewarded James and me with two popsicles from the fridge. We put them on the counter for a split second. The next thing I know, Peppi was holding them sideways on the window ledge. The pops were too heavy for him to hold straight up, so he held the sticks upside down and licked them from the bottom. James and I tried to grab the pops back, but that little white-headed thing opened his mouth and again reminded us of his sharp fangs. Later, Mom asked us how we enjoyed the pops. What the hell could we say?

Peppi also had some peculiar cleaning habits. Mom would cut an onion into quarters. Peppi would pick one up and then start chewing until the juices flowed. He'd rub himself down, eyes full of tears. The onion juice gave him a shiny coat and also seemed to keep the bugs away. When we watched the ritual, James and I would say "yuk!" while Mom would shower praise on the little guy, "What a smart Peppi."

The more mischievous Peppi became, the more he got away with. One time, Mom, Pop, my brother, sister, and I came home from a school event, and the thing is sitting on a mound of freshly made cupcakes. "How fair is that," I protested.

"Arthur," said Mom, "he's only a monkey. What do you expect?"

Pop understood the dilemma right from the outset. A few days after Peppi arrived, he was showing the pet to his buddy Alex in the garage. Alex decides to look closer. "How cute." Peppi grabbed the glasses off the guy's face faster than you could shake a stick and then threw them on the driveway, shattering the lenses. Pop volunteered to buy his friend replacement lenses, but the story never reached Mom's ears. He knew if he ever complained about Peppi, she'd have his ass.

~

I could live with being a second-class son if it wasn't for those damn bites. It seemed whenever we sat down for dinner, Peppi got pissed about not having his own plate and chair. He'd wave his arms, wander around the kitchen, and then slip under the tablecloth. Mom would laugh. Every so often, Peppi used his fangs to bite James and me in the leg. Snake bites take a few seconds before the pain starts flowing. Peppi's bites hurt immediately.

This nonsense went on for months. Mom ignored the biting, but she knew it had to stop. She tried a lot of tricks including not letting the thing in the house when we ate. But, no matter what Mom tried, Peppi wouldn't stop. Eventually, it became obvious—even to Mom—that Peppi, her favorite son, had to go. I'm guessing Pop also finally said something.

To this day, I've got fang scars from the times that little sucker wrapped his arms around my thighs and chomped on my legs.

If your child ever asks for a little white-headed pet monkey, I'd adamantly refuse and offer to buy him a baby tiger cub instead.

Chapter 8

102 Pound Tiger

*Tough little Ernestine Lily Mae, AKA Mom,
made big, bad Art look like a wimp.*

MY POP WAS THE BADDEST guy I knew.

He had arms the size of sewer pipes and a foreboding stare to match. Nobody messed with big Art! But little Ernestine, God bless all 102 pounds of her, pushed his ass around like he was an ant!

Brother James and I figured out pretty early in life that there was only one way to avoid a thrashing from Pop when you did something wrong…get Mom on your side.

A lot of people made the mistake of thinking she was frail and weak. Pound for pound, she was the toughest person I ever knew. She also taught me to stand up for myself. She used to say, "If you don't take care of yourself, who will?"

~

Spanky found that out the hard way.

I was about 16 and was taking this girl—a honey by the name of Vicky—to the weekly Friday night dance on the handball courts. I remember the spot vividly since it was an odd place for a dance. You had to walk along an asphalt path that led to an opening in an eight-foot high chain-link fence to get there.

Vicky was drop-dead gorgeous, and I had developed a real crush on her. So naturally, I wanted to impress her. I even bought her flowers for the dance. Before I knew it, Spanky, the unofficial school bully with this ridiculous nickname, strutted over and started trash talking in front of Vicky. You know stuff like "She should have been able to do a lot better than you," "Where did you get those rags you're wearing," etc.

At six-feet-something and 230 pounds plus, Spanky towered over me although I was no midget myself. I now stood about 5'10" and weighed 187 pounds. I attempted to be a gentleman and suggested he stop. He ignored me. I looked at Vicky, who figured I was intimidated. Now, I'm pissed. (In those days, it didn't take long for me to lose my temper). I remember Pop telling me, "*If you're going to get into a fight, you might as well throw the first punch. It will surprise 'em and sometimes intimidate them to the point of no return.*"

As per Pop, I decided to employ the element of surprise to level the playing field. I hocked a loogie (urban dictionary definition for a large slimy glob of spit, mixed with nose snot, and formed by coughing and hocking up what's in your throat). The loogie was so big, a few of my friends standing nearby became *loogie collateral damage.* Spanky was humiliated by the surrounding laughter. I gave Spanky a knuckle sandwich by throwing the first three or four punches. I can still hear my knuckles crack and the see the pained look on his face as he collapsed. On his way down, I kicked him in the stomach for good measure. He crumpled up like a ball and gasped for air. I figured, what the hell, might as well kick him a few more times for good measure.

I noticed Vicky was shaking like a leaf. I tried to comfort her. (I didn't realize, she'd frightened to death by me, not Spanky).

"Nothing to worry about. It's over." We're now surrounded by lots of kids. The security guards arrived and cuffed me to the chain link fence. Old Spanky was still on the ground, groaning, moaning, and getting more than his share of catcalls.

"He started it," I said.

The guard looked at Sparky, then me. "You're big Art's son right?"

"Yes, sir."

The guard laughed. "The apple doesn't fall far from the tree."

"Look kid, we don't need any more trouble here." Then escorted each of us through the chain link fence... separately.

To my surprise, Vicky wanted to have anything else to do with me. I tried to explain, "I was defending your honor as well as mine!" She wasn't interested. Next thing got a ride home with one of her girlfriends.

I called her a few times after that for a date, but she was always "busy." About the fourth busy, I got the message. I knew I had Spanky to thank for that.

On the plus side, I impressed a lot of my other classmates that evening. In fact, whenever one of my friends needed help, they seemed to summon me for support. I hardly ever created a dispute, but I became a damn good closer.

About 20 years later, I was selling insurance at the Auto Club, when a guy who looked vaguely familiar entered. He said, "Aren't you Arthur Mercado?" I responded, "Who wants to know?" with my usual friendly glare.

The guy smiled. "The last time I saw you, you were handcuffed to the chain-link fence by the handball courts." We laughed. The guy said, "You were such a hothead I thought you'd be dead by now."

You know *I never liked fighting, I just wanted to hurt less than the other guy.*

~

A week after my fourth Vicky call, I was grocery shopping with Mom at Albertson's. We came out of the store with a full cart. Spanky and three of his friends were sitting in the car next to Moms. I figured we're in for some trouble. I told Mom to step aside. I was determined not to lose a fight in front of her.

Spanky was the first to get out of the car. He headed right for me brandishing an 18-inch brass pipe. I knew he's going to try to bash me in the head. I ducked and swung with all my might at his midsection. The force of my blow sent him backward. But not before he threw the pipe at me. It grazed my eye and opened a superficial cut that began to gush crimson. As he got off the ground, there was blood everywhere.

His three buddies decided to join the fray. Mom stopped them in their tracks with the grocery cart. She shouted angrily, "Stay out of it." They stopped in their tracks. That split second gave me the opening I needed. I crushed Spanky again and again. I sat on top of him throwing punch after punch. The force of my blows caused his right ear to scrape the pavement. I kept wailing at him, until a sliver of his ear ground off. He was practically lifeless. Little Ernestine pulled me off and said, "Arthur, you've made your point, now load the groceries in the car."

As she drove, she noticed my eye was bleeding like a pig. She decided to stop at the emergency room on the way home to get me a few stitches. An hour later, we were back in the car heading home. Mom didn't say much, except to make sure I took the groceries out of the car. Once she unpacked, she looked at this bloody mess called her son. "Arthur, throw those clothes away, and go get in the tub, so we can clean you down and soak you in some Epsom salts."

As the blood washed down the drain, I said, "Mom, I'm sorry about today."

She just smiled and said, "Why? You certainly kicked his ass."

I still have a memento from that day: a scar just below my eyebrow where Spanky's pipe hit me.

That Spanky was one dumb mother.

He never bothered me again. But he picked on the wrong guy once too often. About a week later, he was taunting another kid. The way I heard it, the kid pulled out a knife and stabbed Spanky to death. Upon hearing of my buddy's demise, I thought to myself, I was such a nice guy, I only beat him up a little.

~

The "rumble at Sears" was another vintage Mom memory. Pop had given her a few extra bucks to buy something for herself. I went along for the ride because she rarely splurged on herself, so I thought it would be fun to watch her shop.

The traffic was heavy in and out of the lot. It was a Saturday morning. Some chubby 170-pound lady in a white sedan cut in front of Mom as she headed for a parking space. My Mom beeped her horn once and shook her head, "Some people are always in a hurry going nowhere." Next thing I know that lady made the biggest mistake of her life. She gave Mom the finger. Mom's nostrils belched smoke. Next thing I knew, we were flying across the parking lot after the lady with Mom yelling out the window.

The lady must have thought Mom was a mad woman. She pulled her car up on the sidewalk outside the store and started running toward the door. Mom did likewise and started chas- ing her down the sidewalk, "Give me the finger, will you? I'll kick your sorry ass!" I just cracked up. As Mom continued chasing the lady, a whole bunch of shoppers stopped to watch what was going on.

I finally caught up to Mom a few steps inside the store. I grabbed her around the waist. It took every ounce of my now 200-plus pounds to restrain her. As I held her around the waist, she kept yelling, and her feet kept moving. I could see the chubby lady, now frightened to death, hiding in the corner of the store. It took five minutes to calm Mom down.

"Is it safe to let you go? I asked. She nodded.
Everybody
in the store, except that lady, cracked up.

Mom decided she didn't feel like going shopping, so we got
back in the car and headed home. While we were riding, I had a flashback and started chuckling to myself. Mom asked, "What's so funny?" I responded, "I was just thinking about oatmeal."

She smiled, "Got away with that one, huh?"

As a kid, Mom just thought oatmeal was a Louisiana super food. Yup, oatmeal. She'd simmer a big pot until it looked like crud dust, then place it in your dish and tell you how good it was for you. I hated the stuff, but Mom insisted on making it practically every day.

One day, I had decided enough was enough. She turned her head long enough for me to scoop the stuff into my pocket. Then after a "yummy, yummy," I was off to school. Once I got past the neighbor's yard, I dumped the stuff in a clearing.

This went on for quite some time. Mom didn't catch on, the neighbors didn't notice the oatmeal dung, and apparently, it didn't kill any of the local raccoons. To cover my tracks, when I got home, I'd hide the evidence by placing my pants in the middle of a pile of dirty laundry.

One day when I went out to play with my friends after school, Mom decided to do the laundry. Apparently, the oat- meal hardened in the pocket, and Mom had a heck of a time getting the stuff out! But she was pretty cool. She didn't say much at dinner that evening. Just, "Arthur, what was that ter- rible stuff in your pocket?"

I held my breath.

"Sorry, Mom, I'll be more careful about the bubble gum and candy in the future."

Dad looked at me, James looked at me, and Mom looked
at me.

We all smiled. I knew I had just received a free pass.

I'm not sure that lady in Sears would have believed Mom possessed that kind of compassion.

~

Mom taught me a lot of things, but two things stand out in my mind above all else:

The size of your heart has nothing to do with the size of your body.

Be kind and gentle with people, unless they give you shit. Then be prepared to kick their ass.

Chapter 9

Two-Pound Chile Relleño

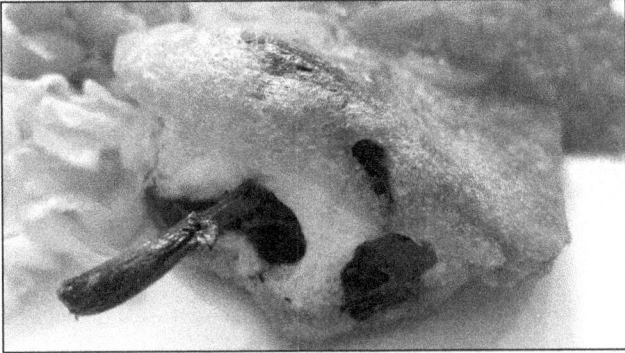

Pop's favorite Mexican repast,
a super-sized Chile Relleño burrito with extra hot sauce.

IT WAS SATURDAY. For whatever reason, Pop suggested we go out to lunch.

Since this wasn't a usual pattern, I jumped at the chance. Assumed he might have had something important he wanted to discuss. Since I a few weeks shy of 16, I thought the concept of car ownership might be on the table.

"Mexican okay?" Pop asked. There was this restaurant Pop loved not far from our house run by three chubby little Mexican ladies.

I nodded. "Doesn't make any difference to me."

The place itself was a little hole in the wall. A small counter that sat six or eight, and three tables behind the counter. But the food was fresh; they were flexible—you could eat in or take out, and the portions were enormous. Pop always equated food quality with food quantity. The house specialty was burritos. These ladies made the biggest burritos I ever saw, then or since.

Not unimportantly, the ladies always laughed at Pop's jokes, which he delivered in a most engaging combination of English and Spanish.

As soon as we entered, they started chatting with Pop in Spanish. The women and Pop were like family. Unfortunately, I didn't speak much Spanish, and I understood even less. I decided to look at the menu.

Pop pointed to me with a big smile. They ladies smiled and nodded. I figured he told the ladies I was his son. The four of them started discussing the menu—in Spanish. One of them pointed, Pop nodded. She then walked over to the kitchen window and said something that sounded like a Chile Relleño burrito. The guy came to the window and responded with a question and a raised eyebrow. She pointed to me and smiled. The guy smiled, shook his head and went back to his stove.

"The specialty here is Chile Relleño burrito," said Pop. "Got one for you and one for me. That okay?"

"Fine."

"Also, got us a couple of large Cokes with ice. Hot as hell today."

A few minutes later two enormous platters arrived. The burritos looked large enough for a school of whales. I figured they weighed two pounds. The burrito was surrounded by a mountain of refried beans and rice.

Pop just started eating. He took a huge bite. I did likewise. It was deeeelicious! I noticed out of the corner of my eye, the three women and the cook were all staring at me. Suddenly, my mouth burst into flames. There was enough heat in that burrito to warm a good-sized house on a cold winter day!

Pop waited for me to yell, *no mas*, but there was no way I was going to give him that satisfaction. I sipped some of the cold Coke, which only made the heat more intense. I smiled. "Damn good burrito, Pop."

He was dumbfounded at my cool, calm and collective response, but he kept a poker face. I took another bite and then another. I was sweating like a pig. At one point, I thought I might pass out.

The ladies started yelling something to my father. He waved them away. We were clearly in the midst of a "Mexican standoff." I sat there and ate the entire smokin' burrito.

I tried to make conversation with Pop to take my mind off what I was doing. He just answered with one-word responses. "Yup, nope, maybe." I have no idea what I tried to say.

When we finished, he paid the check, and we headed back to the car. It was about 100 degrees, but my stomach is at least 20 degrees hotter.

Pop never said anything more about the incident. But I know I made him proud.

When a man can handle anything that's handed him without complaining, he officially becomes a man.

Chapter 10
Standoff @ Los Altos

Celebrating my newly found independence in my chick-mobile.

POP THOUGHT I WAS out of my mind.

But to me, it was straightforward. I had survived my first two years at Los Altos High School and put up with all the crap that befalls an underclassman. I was comin' round the bend to my junior and senior years when all the good stuff happened.

I didn't want to start over again at another school. But, Pop had decided. He and Mom were off to live in Yucaipa, initially in a trailer, and then to wherever. "Mom and I want to get away from the city."

Lori and James just went along. But Pop and I debated the issue…at least as far as Pop would allow one of his kids to debate. He could see I was the "odd child out."

"Okay, tough guy, you want to live in the house and graduate from Los Altos?"

Without hesitation, I responded, "Yes, sir." In our house, if you didn't answer "yes sir" or "no sir" you would get a knuckle sandwich.

"You understand, I'm not about to support you," he glared.

I know I'm dangerously close to pushing the buttons of the only man I knew who could single-handedly kick a gorilla's ass. "Yes, sir."

"So you are going to pay all the house bills?"

"Yes, sir."

"And, the payments on that damn car?"

"Yes, sir."

"And, finish high school?"

"Yes, sir."

Pop could see the determination in my eyes. "Fine then. But you miss one payment, fail one course, and you're out. Understand."

"I understand."

That standoff was my first taste of adult poker. Pop didn't argue; I'm certain he figured I was bluffing, and that I'd eventually fold. He probably assumed I'd drop out of Los Altos and come begging.

I saw the cards a little differently. I had made a deal. If I wanted to keep my dignity, I knew I could never retreat. I had to fulfill my part of the bargain. *Once you make a commitment to something, there's no backpedaling.*

Next thing I know, I'm going to school, doing homework, and driving an hour each way from Los Altos High to Pasadena to work a full shift at a promotional marketing company. It was not the most exciting job in the world—I mostly ran the addressograph machine to label flyers. But, it paid the bills, and that was all that mattered. Occasionally, I got assigned to do the midnight mail run. That was a euphemism for driving the company van filled with bulk advertising flyers 30 minutes to the Los Angeles Central Post Office.

~

I liked the midnight run because there was no traffic by LA standards. I decided to ask the boss if I could earn a little overtime money by adding an after-hours run to my regular duties. He agreed, and the bucks started to roll in.

At least, until *that night.* I'm driving over a two-lane bridge south of Los Angeles when I notice two street gangs shouting, arguing and pushing each other at the far end of the bridge. I come to a dead stop, leaving the truck to idle.

The gangs were looked about to get it on—I could see the shiny switch blades. Suddenly one of gang leaders spotted this lone truck driven by a white guy (me). He yelled something to both sides. Suddenly everybody charged toward me screaming in Spanish. Best I could tell, it was something about *killing THE gringo.* I was certain they were going to force me to stop, steal the truck's contents, and beat the shit out of me, not necessarily in that order.

I thought about making a sharp U-Turn. but there was neither the time or room. My only option was straight ahead. I stepped on the gas and headed straight for the crowd, horn beeping. My heart was pounding. One guy bounced off the side of the truck. They disbursed big time. I never looked back.

I got to the post office in record time, did my business, and drove the hell home! From that day forward, I decided to work in the shop rather than drive through the Stiletto Ghetto. The boss was cool. He still gave me extra work.

The good news is that thanks to the overtime, I paid every bill on time and completed my studies. I also learned another valuable life lesson: *bravery among street gangs is for chumps unless you have a distinct advantage.*

Chapter 11

Poker Hooky

William Tarr, the Dean who almost did me in.

THE WEEKLY POKER GAME was going well.

I had won the last three hands; and my classmates, Lee Strollo, Mike Tucker, and Jeff Walsh, were taking it in the shorts. It's about 2 p.m. We had decided to play hooky that day. I called the school and said I had a sore throat and a touch of the flu which might be contagious. Since I lived alone without parents, the school nurse had no way to challenge my excuse.

In separate calls, Strollo impersonated his father who explained Lee twisted his ankle badly at track practice. I'm not sure how the other guys got out of class. How everybody got there didn't matter to me. All that mattered was in another few hours, my buds would be broke, and I would celebrate their losses by taking them to dinner. *Hey, isn't that's what friends are for?*

~

The doorbell rang. Unfortunately, playing hooky was a bit more complicated for the other guys. They couldn't just forge their parents' signature because they still lived at home and had to answer to their parents when the Dean or his assistant made his verification call.

There's a loud knock on the door. Then another. I peeked out the window from behind the curtain. There stood the nerdy-looking Dean of Boys, Mr. Tarr.

Everybody was parked around the cul-de-sac adjacent to my house, and we had been playing a few hours, so there are cards, money, and drinks everywhere. "It's Tarr," I whispered. Within a matter of moments, the boys cleaned the place cleaned up and were hiding in the bedroom down the hall.

I slowly opened the door, feigning illness. "Sir, sorry I didn't answer sooner. I was in bed when I heard the knock."

Mr. Tarr glared skeptically, "I gather you're not feeling well today, Arthur?"

"No sir, sick as a dog. Flu or something. Also, got some terrible cramps in my stomach."

The guy scanned the living room. He saw the table with a few cards and the money accidentally left behind. I'm quiet as a church mouse

He said, "How are Lee, Mike, and Jeff feeling? I gather from the school nurse everybody's a little under the weather."

I put on my best poker face. "I think they're coping'. What makes you ask, sir?"

"Oh, there just seemed to be a lot of cars parked at the end of your cul-de-sac in the middle of the day." You could hear the gasps in the bedroom. Tarr shook his head and smiled stoically. "Gotta hand it to you guys, you've certainly got balls." He then walked towards the door, and stopped. "I assume you'll all feel better by tomorrow."

I know for a fact he wrote notes to my parents and my friends parents to complain about my behavior. But, Mom and Dad lived quite a distance, so they never responded. And, my grades were darn good, so there really wasn't much else he could. But, Mr. Tarr had made his point. That was our last weekday poker game. That little incident taught me to *never underestimate the observational powers of so-called cool nerds.*

~

It was the Wednesday before graduation.

I called home. Pop answered.

"What are you guys doing Saturday?"

"Nothing in particular," said Pop.

"Would you like to come to my ceremony?"

"What ceremony?"

"My high school graduation ceremony." That was how I broke the news that I had kept my end of the bargain.

There was dead silence on the other end of the phone. The phone fell to the floor. In the background, I hear Mom ask Pop, "Arthur, what's the matter?" Again, dead silence.

Mom picked up the phone. "Hello. Who is this?" I tell Mom I am graduating and want them to come to the ceremony. They came. But, Pop didn't say much. What a surprise! I could read his eyes. He was *proud of my accomplishments, and that made me feel good.* At that point, I didn't even care there was no graduation present.

~

After high school, I decided to attend Citrus Community College in Glendora to further my education. The Vietnam War was starting to hit high gear, and I wanted to make something of myself.

Pop and Mom decided to sell the Los Altos house, so I rented a little old Cape Cod style house in the center of Glendora that was within walking distance of the college. I had used most of my high school earnings to keep my end of the deal with Pop, so all I could afford was a beat-up '58 Chevy. But, my friends who knew the deal I made with my Pop thought it was "cool" that I beat the old man at his game.

I guess that whole experience taught me another lesson: *if you're going to try to win by bluffing, you better have a solid backup plan, just in case.*

~

In my first semester, I received a 3.4 grade-point average (out of 4.0), which was damn good considering I worked full time during the day and went going to school at night until about 10 p.m. before completing homework assignments. I remember proudly mailing that first report card to Pop with no note.

Nothing happened. No call. No congratulations note. I'm a little disappointed.

About two weeks later, Pop showed up unannounced with the coolest car I had ever seen. A candy-apple green, fully refurbished 1955 Ford with green tuck and roll seats, new carpet, and new stereo.

"Transmission, rear end, and engine have all been reworked," said Pop. "Go look."

I opened the hood. It was amazing. A three-power manifold with three gleaming chrome 97S two-barreled carburetors stood at attention. Everything that could be covered in chrome was covered in chrome. Even the top of the radiator was polished brass.

"Mom thought you deserved it."

"You mean it's mine?"

"Got a good deal on it," he said stoically. "There are no payments to make." (Turned out a guy he worked with had spent two years refurbishing it with his son before he died of a sudden heart attack. The son just wanted to get rid of it. The memories were too sad).

I looked in the back seat.

"What's that?"

"TV."

"For who?"

"You got one?"

"No."

"Well, then."

Like I said before, Pop wasn't much for words.

He left. I felt great. It was his way of saying he loved me. I opened the TV box. It even had a remote control, which at the time was the latest rage.

I thought to myself. The un-cool high school kid wound up with the coolest car and the coolest TV.

Lesson learned: Sometimes, cool just comes to those who wait.

Chapter 12

Imaginary Steady

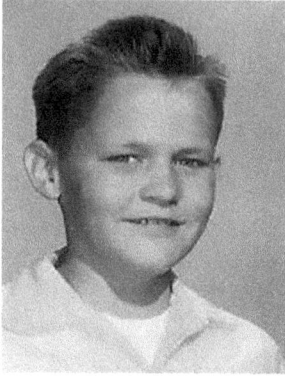

Leslie Thomas was my first love even though she ignored me.

I WAS CRAZY ABOUT LESLIE from the first time I laid eyes on her in the sixth grade. She was hands down, the cutest girl in school. She had a smile that could light up a room.

By the eighth grade, I imagined she was my girlfriend, although I had never asked her out, and she had never expressed even the slightest interest talking to me. As it turned out, that was the *high point of our relationship.*

A few weeks after high school began at Los Altos, I decided I'd make my move. Unfortunately for me, Leslie started being wooed by upperclassmen, like juniors and seniors. Suddenly, I felt like a dirt clog.

To make matters worse, I was big and gawky for my age, and not exactly the sharpest dressed kid in school. (Pop had stretched to purchase our new three-bedroom home for about $8,000, so there wasn't much left over after mortgage payments and expenses for the latest fashions). My awkward appearance was frequently noted in the halls by the older boys, which in turn made me even more self-conscious. It became an effort for me to speak to any of the girls I thought were good-looking because I always felt I was one sentence away from being humiliated.

Over the long haul, those difficult times taught me something important. *It makes no sense to moan about the bad hand you've been dealt. Nobody cares! And, here's the best part, only you can make it right.*

~

Despite my little bumps in the road, I remained crazy about Leslie. I could feel my heart race whenever she passed. And, when she gave me even a casual glance, I felt like the proverbial knight in shining armor. On those rare occasions when she stopped to chat, I felt like Denny Dimwit, I could barely string two coherent sentences together.

One day I was sitting in the stands watching the cheerleaders practice. Leslie glided through her routine. I imagined she was smiling at me. After they had finished, she was standing with a small group of other cheerleaders. "That's was great," I said. She smiled warmly. "Thanks." I thought that was my moment. Awkwardly I asked her if she'd like to go to the movies. Her girlfriends snickered. I was rejected on the spot. But, she was nice about it. "Sorry, I don't date underclassmen."

Her rejection confirmed what I thought for quite some time; I lacked "California coolness." Despite this obvious shortcoming, I managed to find a few guys like me, and they became my high school world. At that point my life my goals were rather limited—I simply wanted to reach senior year so that I could hang out in the space between a gym and the main classroom building. And, maybe get another shot at Leslie.

Eventually, I would make it to senior year but never dated Leslie. That experience taught me something important: *If you get rejected in matters of the heart, don't sweat it. Rejection is a part of life, like peanut butter and jelly, and croutons and Caesar salad.*

Chapter 13

Who Me?

My unexpected prom date, the most beautiful and popular girl in school.

WITH MY OPPOSITE-SEX insecurities, girls were not exactly lining up to accept my invitation to the senior prom. In fact, I had pretty much decided there was no way I was going. (It never occurred to me, until years later, that my perpetual scowl and peculiar sense of humor might have been a turn-off).

Despite my awkwardness around girls, I still considered myself a social animal. I liked people and wanted to be around them. Consequently, I decided prom or no prom, my friends and I would have a blowout "unchaperoned" post-prom keg party at my house for 20 or so of my best friends

~

It was a sunny day about two weeks before the prom. I'm was hanging out in the senior space. Along came Pamela Siegel and a few of her girlfriends. Pamela was not only prettiest girl in school, but she was also smart, self-confident, and very sexy. She started to flirt with my buddy Art, who considered himself quite the ladies' man.

Pamela attracted boys like a bee collected honey. Same with rumors. It was general knowledge that Pamela had a "loose" streak when it came to boys. But, nobody who dated her was willing wouldn't admit to anything unless they had a few too many beers!

~

To everyone's surprise, this nerdy little guy we used to call John the Scientist walked up to Pamela and flat out asked her to be his date at the senior prom.

She looked at him condescendingly. "Please, you must be kidding." Then she turned her back. She and her girlfriends began snickering loudly. The nerd walked away dejected and humiliated. I felt sorry for the guy, but I just keep talking to my friends. I figured the nerd would ultimately come to grips with his rejection so long as my buddies didn't rub any additional salt into his wounds.

Next thing I knew, there was a tap on my shoulder. It was Pamela with a seductive smile on her face. "Arthur, would you be my date to the prom?"

I was blown away! I didn't even think she knew my name. I'm thinking, *Leslie, help. I'm crazy about you. Where are you? Why aren't you asking me?* Instead, I said, "Who me?"

She smiled, rolled her eyes and said simply, "Yes, you."

I melted. The blurted out, "Sure, why not."

"Call me so we can discuss the details." She handed me her phone number then walked away.

Art gave me the old "right on." He assumed I would score big.

Pamela had just taught me an important lesson about relationships. *When you act cool—even accidentally—it greases cupid's arrows.*

~

I don't remember much about the actual prom, other than I was a perfect gentleman. I bought Pamela a nice corsage— she smelled great—we had lots of laughs at dinner then danced the twist and stuff until the band shut down.

When we got to her door, she put her arms around me, moved her lips close to my face, and closed her eyes. I just said goodbye without even trying to kiss her. She was speechless. I don't think anybody had ever passed on her advances.

As I walked away, she said, "Where are you going in such a hurry?"

I explained some my friends were on the way over to my house for a keg party, and I wanted to be there when they arrived.

In case you were wondering, no, I never dated Pamela again.

~

The other thing I realized somewhat later was that *all the beer in the world with all the friends in the world, may not be as rewarding as an evening with the most willing girl in the world!*

Chapter 14

Diane & Me

Diane and her fashionable beehive at the senior prom.

I CAN STILL REMEMBER how Diane and I became an item.

It was a Saturday afternoon and I was heading home in my shiny little Triumph to pick up my poker buddy, Mike Tucker. We planned to stop at this popular new fast food place called In-N-Out Burger on Francisquito Avenue. A dark blue 4-door Chevrolet idled at the traffic light heading in the opposite direction. I noticed Diane sitting in the back seat behind her father. I accelerated real slow, looked in her open window, and smiled. She smiled back. I melted.

It was really my lucky day! As Mike and I wolfed down our burgers, I discovered he had Diane's home phone number since he was good friends with her older brother.

At 3 p.m. I called. At 7 p.m. I picked her up.

That first date was nothing fancy. Sandwiches and donuts at a local diner, then we just drove around talking. Man was she fun. She had this dry sense of humor that matched me to a tee. I knew she was the one. Before long we were a real item. We did lots of stuff together: I escorted her to her prom where we danced the Swing and Lindy, plus a few slow songs where I could feel her nuzzle up to me. Life was good and simple! We went to parties and clubs, listened to Elvis and the Beach Boys, and walked on the beach some nights. What I learned with Diane was that some things were just mean to be.

Diane was a good dancer, but she was a great kisser! Her older brother had just graduated with me. As Diane walked across the field with her family to congratulate her brother I just grabbed her and gave her a big kiss. She was surprised, but loved it. Her parents weren't amused. *I guess I've always believed you should do what you want, when you want, so long as you're not hurting somebody.*

~

By the time Diane graduated, I had a full-time job as a mechanic's helper and a was renting a little one-bedroom house not far from Citrus College where I had enrolled. So, we did more grown up things like going to the Ice House in Pasadena to watch the stand-up comics who were trying to make it in the "Big Time." I don't remember the name of one comic, but I do remember how we laughed and laughed. I took her to see Johnny Mathis at the Greek Theater (she loved his singing) among other places. Diane was always such a lady, she just naturally taught me to be a gentleman around women, without ever saying a word.

In the beginning, I picked her up at her house. But it didn't take me long to figure out Diane's father didn't think I was the right choice for his daughter. My reputation for finishing too many fights (that was true) preceded me. He also didn't like what he called my "smug" attitude. (that was not true). I think he gave me that label after I helped him fix his car. The engine was misfiring badly. I told him what we needed to do to the carburetor. He disagreed.

Two hours later, we did it my way and the car started purring. He was a big dude, maybe six-two or three, so he just stared at me. Don't remember exactly what I said about his mechanical prowess, but he didn't find it funny.

It was different story when Diane came to dinner at my parents' house. Big Art and Ernestine thought Diane was the coolest young lady. She quickly grew to like my parents too!

~

As our relationship progressed, we began to have intimate relations at my place, but she always went home. She had a curfew and wanted to abide by her parents' rules. At that stage of our relationship, we were, as Forest Gump said about his Jenny, "like peas and carrots."

One night Diane came by the house and mentioned she was feeling "queasy." I said, "maybe you're just hungry," and then made her some scrambled eggs. She ate most of it but still was not feeling right. I joked, "maybe you're pregnant!" We talked about it and said she could be, but not sure and then she headed home.

After she left, I started to think about the what if's. Suppose she was pregnant? What should I do? What was I supposed to do? What did I want to do? After going to a party one night, I never called her again. Sadly, I did nothing about the possibly she could be pregnant.

~

About six or seven months later—*yes six or seven months*— I'm driving in my car when Diane driving beside me at a stop light. I couldn't help but notice how big her stomach was. Again, I didn't say or do anything, even though I loved her like crazy.

About a month or so later, Diane delivered a baby girl. I heard through the grapevine that my flesh and blood was going to be put up for adoption. I knew I had to right the ship. I called Diane at the hospital. She agreed to meet.

Unbeknownst to Diane, I went to the viewing room. I saw my daughter for the first time. The nurse let me hold her. My brain had trouble processing everything. Hard to put into words, even today. Later, I told Diane I had seen our daughter, and wanted to support her, but I don't think I ever mentioned marriage. Big mistake! She said no. I stared for a moment then turned around and left.

Later that day, without Diane's knowledge, I met with her father and explained my intentions. I asked for Diane's hand in marriage. His response was short and sweet, "Over my dead body." I offered to support the baby and let things with Diane quiet down. Again, he shook his head, "thanks but no thanks," and showed me the door. I never stepped foot in that house again. And, worse still, I never called Diane again, and she never called me.

Sometime later I received a draft notice in the mail. The Vietnam war had heated up. It never occurred that 50 years would pass before I'd see Diane again!

Everybody makes stupid decisions as we pass through life. But you better figure out how to fix them, otherwise you may die one unhappy dude.

Chapter 15

Sergeant Mercado

vs.

Private Mercado

Recruits never win in the army. But I did. Eventually.

POP ONLY HUGGED ME ONCE and cried in front of me once.

It was June 1967. I had been drafted into the Army. He took me to report. We were both concerned about the possibility of me winding up in Vietnam. It was not a very good place to be.

As we stood outside his car, he gave me a big hug and said, "I love you."

"Me too, Pop," I responded.

He wiped the tears from his eyes, got in his car, and drove away. I'm sure he thought he'd never see me again.

That was the last bit of tenderness I was to experience for some time.

~

Anybody that's been in the army knows the drill.

Basic training is designed to break you down and then build you up. You're essentially a piece of dung! I'm assigned to this company where the 1st Lieutenant was hell bent to make Captain. It was mess time. Everybody stacked their rifles on the rack.

"Private Mercado," said my platoon sergeant, Sergeant Young.

"Yes, Sergeant."

"You're the sentry."

"Yes, Sergeant."

While I was standing guard along came the Company Commander.

I saluted him. He walked by then stopped and turned. I had a bad feeling. He walked into my face. "Did you just salute me at parade rest, you dumb, stupid so and so?" (You're supposed to stand at attention when saluting an officer. I made an honest mistake).

His tone said it all. I knew I was doomed from that moment forward.

Whenever he saw me, he trumped up some violation and forced me to do push-ups in front of everybody. One time, he ran into me in the mess hall. He made me put my tray on the floor, complete 30 push ups, and eat my meal at the same time. I arrived for basic training at 220 pounds. Six weeks later, I was 197 pounds.

The continued harassment by my Sergeant and the CO pissed me off. I could feel the rage building inside of me. But I kept my mouth shut. That's how you played the game.

One day, my Sergeant and I walked down the hall in the building that housed the CO. Another platoon sergeant with my last name walked by. "Hey, Sgt. Mercado," said Sergeant Young. "This your son?" pointing to my name tag. A flip switched on in my brain. I mumble, "He wouldn't make the dong on my old man."

Sgt. Young knew I had made a big mistake. So did Sgt. Mercado. The next thing I know, the three of us are pushing and shoving outside the commander's office. Hearing the commotion, the CO stomped into the hallway. "What the hell is going on?"

Sgt. Mercado and Sgt. Young explained their version of what had transpired. I wasn't asked for my side of the story, but there was not much I could say anyway.

The commanding officer pulled me into his office and said, "Private, your disorderly outburst has just earned you an article 15 (a minor smudge on your military record), loss of pay and extra duty for thirty days."

For some reason, I remembered what my brother James told me before I left for basic training. "If you ever get an article fifteen, demand a court martial. It's your right." Officers knew a court martial proceeding was a red flag. It suggested chaos within the ranks, which was not a positive event for anyone seeking promotion.

"Sir, I respectfully refuse the article 15 and request a court martial."

The CO tried to intimidate me.

"You stupid excuse for a man, you know what you're requesting?"

"Yes, sir," I said.

He tried to negotiate. "Okay, an article fifteen, loss of pay, and extra duty for fifteen days.

I remained at attention. Like Pop told me, *when you smell fear that's the best time to attack your opponent.* "Sir, Private Mercado still respectfully requests a court martial."

The officer was forced to decide. My court martial or his potential promotion.

"Mercado, get the hell out of here, but I never want to hear about you again. Do we understand each other?"

"Yes, sir."

During the last few weeks of boot camp, I didn't do another push-up either.

Chapter 16
Five-Month Vet

*I entered the service in January and was honorably discharged in May,
a record for military stupidity.*

IT WAS ABOUT 1 P.M. We'd been drilling on the
parade grounds at Ford Ord in Monterey, California. I
was about four months and six days into my two-year
tour of duty.

I'd developed quite a blister on my heel. I tried to
shake it off, but it was becoming increasingly difficult to
execute the platoon's typical marching exercises. The
discomfort was so bad I had to do the unthinkable! I
requested a conversation with our drill sergeant to explain
my predicament. Not surprisingly, he didn't believe me.
He told me to take off my boot. "Let's see the f...ing
leg," he growled.

After examining the swelling, he commanded me to
change into my low quarters and "get your butt back
here."

I did as ordered. The blister got worse. My ankle
swelled up like a grapefruit, and the skin hung over my
low quarters.

I got a shooting pain in my hip. The drill sergeant continued to believe I was dogging it. "Drop your pants, private."

The squad snickered.

The sergeant saw a red line heading up my leg to my groin. He knew it was abnormal, but that's about it. "Soldier, get yourself to the damn dispensary!" he shouted.

The place was a mile or more away; I started dragging my leg down the street. Some regular-duty soldiers in a pickup truck noticed me struggling and gave me a ride.

I entered the dispensary and explained the situation. The nurse looked at my leg. I could tell she was alarmed but calm and collected. They quickly soaked my leg in Epsom salts, wrapped it in towels, and stuck it in a plastic bag. My leg got hotter, the pain was throbbing, and the streak was getting redder. Still no doctor.

By now, I'd also developed a good fever, so they started pouring Kool-Aid down my throat and gave me a shot of something. They were sure I had some form of blood poisoning. The nurse said reassuringly, "Soldier if this swelling doesn't go down, we're going to immerse you in a tub of ice." I sensed a growing urgency.

Finally, I was wheeled into something that appeared to be an emergency procedure room. This guy started checking my pulse. "We're going to stick this needle into the middle of the infected area. It may hurt a bit."

My pulse doubled. The needle was inserted. The pain felt like somebody shot a bazooka up my ass! But the fever subsided, the swelling in my leg went down, and I slept very well that evening.

At 5 a.m., I awoke for a bathroom stop. My back was killing me. I tried to struggle to my feet with little success. A soldier with a mop and bucket tapped me on the shoulder. "Your turn to clean the floors."

I think the guy is crazy; he started to pull my sheet down. I told him to leave me alone. Mercifully, the Colonel of Orthopedic Surgery was making early rounds and heard the dispute. He realized I wasn't dogging it, and told the guy to leave me alone.

Next thing I know, I was being whizzed me down the hall on a gurney into an austere room where they took some x-rays. Then they wheeled me back to my bed. That night, I didn't sleep very well. I heard a few wounded Vietnam vets screaming in agony. And the bedmate on my right was a fount of depressing information. "Heard they left a sponge in the stomach of one guy and a plastic glove in the leg of another...and there was this soldier who was stabbed by his date in a bar. Messed him up pretty good."

It seemed like I just got to sleep when I discovered the Colonel at my bedside. "Soldier," he said, "I've got your test results. You've got some serious disc degeneration."

To say I was shocked would be an understatement. "This just happened?"

"No, from the looks of your spine," he said, "this is a case of chronic deterioration."

He continued. "We've got to operate."

"Operate on what, Sir?"

"If we don't fix your back, you're going to be a cripple by the time you're thirty."

Chapter 17

Trading Ithaca

Pop's favorite. The crème de la crème of shotguns.

POP THOUGHT I SHOULD have my own shotgun. After all, he reasoned if we were going to hunt as a team, each man needed his own equipment. One day, he saw this ad in the classified section "well-kept hunting rifle for sale." The address was a distance out-of-town. "Sounds like it might be a pretty good deal," he said. "Think I'll check it out. Wanna come?"

Next thing I know, Pop and I were in the car heading down the highway. When we finally found the address, it turned out to be a small trailer sitting next to a big sand dune. Parked nearby was an old station wagon, presumably used to haul the trailer. It was a sorry sight with sunbaked paint and tattered seats. Pop guessed it was 20 years old if it was a day.

He knocked on the trailer door. An old man in his eighties stood in front of us. Pop introduced himself and said he was there to consider buying the gun that was advertised.

The man looked out and saw Pop's brand new Ithaca shotgun in the back of his car.

"If you've got one of them, why do you want one of mine?"

Pop responded, "It's for my son. We like to go hunting together."

I could tell Pop's response struck a chord with the old man. He agreed to let us in the trailer. The interior was a hodge-podge.

Pop picked up the rifle. "Seems to be in good firing order."

"What do you expect," said the man crustily. "The damn coyotes and stuff come right up to the door. Gotta be ready."

In short order, Pop discovered the old man lived by himself. His wife had died 15 years earlier. He had no family, no friends to speak of, and from the looks of things, barely enough money to make ends meet.

"That car pull the trailer?" said Pop.

"When I can afford the gas." The man paused, "Who wants to know?"

Pop decided to offer the man some lemonade he had bought along on the way. They sat down and talked for a while, about nothing in particular.

"Damn fine gun, that Ithaca. Seen them ads. Bet it's one expensive piece of hardware."

Pop saw the wistfulness in the old man's eyes. When Pop got home, he started talking about the day's experience. I knew the old man made quite an impression on Pop because Pop rarely talked about his feelings. I remember him reflecting as he sat in his living room chair, "No one should be alone like that. *Arthur, remember as you grow up, no matter how little or how much God gives you, make sure you share.*"

About two weeks later Pop was sitting reading the newspaper when I walked in the room.

He pointed to a Wal-Mart advertisement. "Great price for an Ithaca gun. What say we go shopping in the morning?" I nod, thinking I'm about to get a gift.

Wal-Mart opened at 8 a.m. We arrived around nine. Pop headed straight to the gun counter.

"Like to buy one of those Ithaca guns you advertised.

"Sorry sir," said the man behind the counter, "We're sold out."

Pop was furious. "How could you be sold out? The ad only ran last night?"

The salesman tried to explain something about an early morning run. Pop would hear none of it. The conversation became heated. Pop stuck to his guns, so to speak. In the end, they gave Pop a rain check. When the next shipment arrived, he got the gun at the sale price.

On the ride home he said nothing, I figured he wanted to hold it for a Christmas present.

"Arthur," he smiled the next day, "how about we take another trip to see that old man in the desert?"

I wondered why he wanted to go back out there, but I readily agreed. It was always an adventure being with Pop. He had so much wisdom. I noticed he put that new Ithaca shotgun in the back seat.

We got to the old man's trailer. He invited us in.

"So, what brings you back this way?"

My Pop amazed me. Turned out on our first visit Pop noticed an old rusty hunting rifle leaning against the wall in the corner of the trailer.

"Thinking," said Pop with a twinkle in his eye. "Ever consider trading that gun for my Ithaca straight up?" I think to myself; *Pop's been in the sun too long.*

"Arthur," the old man had learned his name, "you trying to steal my best gun. I may be an old man, but I'm not an old fool."

They haggled for almost an hour. Everybody in the trailer, including me, understood the game. Pop wanted to give the old man his gun. The old man was too proud to accept charity.

Finally, the deal was struck. Pop gave him the new Ithaca and some shells in exchange for the old gun. After they had shaken hands to consummate the deal, the old man smiled and said proudly, "You city boys. I sure got the best of that one."

"How do you know the barrel isn't bent," smiled Pop.

The man nodded. I just knew it was his way of saying thank you without saying thank you. Pop didn't say much on the ride back. He just grinned a lot. "Bet that old guy lives another ten years with that shotgun by his side."

We never saw the old man again. But I was certain of two things: Pop was right about the man's longevity. And *there is a fine line between a demeaning handout and an act of loving generosity.*

Chapter 18

First Time Dying

No athletic endeavor was ever too much for Pop and me,
but hunting was clearly our favorite bonding experience.

HUNTING SEASON ALWAYS rang my chimes.

It was late August, and Pop, James, and I were raring to go. After all, it was the first day of deer season.

It was also hot as hell. At 6 a.m., the thermometer read 95°.

We drove to one of our favorite spots—the top of a hill in Rancho California near the outskirts of the Camp Pendleton Marine Base. The spot was perfect. We had an uninterrupted 360 ° panoramic view. There was not a soul in sight, not even a soldier. My instinct told me the hills were filled with deer.

Pop pointed to the canyon on his right. "I'm guessing we'll find some big boys down that canyon." I responded smugly, "I'm guessing there are more deer down the canyon to the left," pointing in the opposite direction.

Pop tried to convince me that we were safer traveling and hunting as a group. But he was unable to talk sense into his wise-ass son, brimming with self-confidence. We did a little verbal sparring. James started to pull him away, so we don't spoil the day. Pop shook his head. He realized you couldn't reason with a rock! He looked at his watch. "Gonna be a scorcher. Just make sure we meet back here around lunchtime. Don't want anybody to get dehydrated." Shortly after we split up. James and Pop went their way, and I went mine.

No long after, I spotted a dry creek down the bottom of a canyon filled with scrub oak. I figure it might be a good starting point. The climb down was quite steep. There were a number of places where I had to jump down several feet at a time. At that point, I was thinking about am I going to get myself and the deer, I'm certain to bag, back up the canyon.

Time flew. I was totally engrossed in stalking my prey. First, I spotted a doe. That was off-bounds. Finally, I spotted a buck and scoped the sucker. I fired my round and missed. He fled. I searched deeper into the woods. I spotted another buck. This time, I didn't shoot; I decided he was too handsome. It's now almost noon and scorching. I guessed the temperature was 100+ degrees, and I the sweat was pouring off me.

I also discovered I out of water and down to my last four shells. I figured it was time to rendezvous with Pop and James. I started hiking up the creek. I suddenly realized the climb almost impossible. I began to scale my way back up. I never get more than half-way. Each attempt ended with me slipping back down. I tried absolutely everything...from jamming branches into the hillside to hold my position and then digging steps, to crawling on my belly at steep plateaus. Between the heat and the strain, I became light-headed. I must have passed out and fallen some 30 feet straight down.

When I awoke, my rifle lay next to me. Miraculously, I was still in one piece, and so was my rifle.

I tried crawling up the hill, only to fall again. This time on my head. I must have been unconscious for some period. When I woke up, there are lizards crawling all over my face and body. I shook them off and tried desperately to crawl back up the hill several more times.

I passed out several more times. Each time, I experienced a weird dream. I remember them like it was yesterday. First, I'm sucking colorful snow cones in Alabama. Then I'm eating watermelons. My adrenaline reached a fever pitch. When I regained consciousness, I noticed I had stopped sweating. I knew I was dehydrated.

~

Things only got worse. I spotted two or three ravenous coyotes moving in for the kill. I decided to shoot three of my remaining shells in the air to signal for help (the hunter's SOS), hoping against hope that someone, somehow would hear them. Just in case, I decided to save the last bullet for me. I realized if I'm still stuck out here after nightfall, I'm going to get attacked from all sides.

After resting a bit, I was ready to attempt my final ascent in the daylight. I saw a helicopter about two canyons over. I tried yelling, to no avail. The sound of the blades drowned me out. I was completely out of steam. My heart was pounding so hard I could feel it through my shirt. I passed out again.

When I regained consciousness, there was a huge marine helicopter hovering over me with a harness hanging down. A voice yelled, "Put on the harness. Repeat put on the harness."

The blades were probably eight feet away from the side of the mountain, but at my angle of vision, they seemed inches away. I wrapped the harness around me. The marine was screaming, "hurry up." The mountain seemed like it was getting closer.

Suddenly, I realized I had left my rifle on the ground. I dragged myself over to my weapon, stuffed it in the harness, and waved to pull me up. I wasn't about to leave such an expensive piece of equipment behind. As I ascended, I could feel the late afternoon air blow through my hair. The feeling was wonderful.

As they struggled to pull me on board, one of the Marines yelled in my face, "Why were you wasting time retrieving that old gun?" He tossed my Ithaca into the corner of the helicopter and pulled me up.

I tried to crack a joke. "It was a gift from my Pop." The helicopter started to bank. I began to slip out. He grabbed me by the arm. Thank God, he was strong as an ox. He dragged me back aboard as the helicopter sped toward the campground.

As I'm sitting against the wall inside the helicopter, he again gets in my face. "What's the matter with you? Didn't you realize?"

I wondered, realize what? He gave me the answer.

"That guy in the next canyon wasn't so lucky. He didn't make it. I just happened to see you laying there out of the corner of my eye as I was circling to return to base." He continued, "Must not have been your time. You're one sorry, lucky ass!"

~

The ride back seemed like forever. I was barely conscious by the time we arrived at the campgrounds. They carried me to a lounge chair. There was Pop standing over me with a cold bottle of Coca Cola. "Here, stupid!"

I tried drinking it. My throat closed completely. I signaled I was unable to breathe. Pop grabbed some ice. He opened my mouth and stuck a chunk of ice down my throat to open the passage. It worked. I started drinking everything in sight to regain my senses and strength.

When I finally felt strong enough to walk, he took me to the bathroom for a look in the mirror. I don't recognize what I saw: there was this ugly face with a pained expression and two black holes that once held eyes.

"I've seen dead men that look better than you," laughed Pop. "Looks like you drank everything in sight. Ain't none left for anybody else." He then got in his truck and drove to a local general store to restock.

Minutes later, I fell sound asleep. I was a limp dishcloth that slept like a rock. The next morning, I awakened to the bright sun streaming through my window and Pop's confident voice. "Rise and shine. Great day for hunting."

I got dressed, picked up my gun, grabbed a cup of coffee, rolled off the kitchen table, and got in Pop's car. There is absolutely no mention of the day before. It was like the incident never happened. I got the message loud and clear. *When crap happens, you just have to deal with it.*

I also got my first taste of dying. Interesting.

~

A week later, I was back at the same campground. This time with my friend, Jim Thomas, and his father. We went hunting but bagged nothing. We decided to have a drink before we headed home; Jim spotted a squadron of big ass tarantulas walking right past our chairs. He decided to catch a few and put them in a coffee can.

"These guys will make great plastic paperweights," he said.

I thought he was crazy, but who cared. They weren't going to my house.

On the way back, Jim fell fast asleep in the back seat. He dreamt the damn tarantulas hopped out of the can and started crawling up his chest. He started screaming. Mr. Thomas lost control and drove into a ditch. I woke up wondering what the hell was going on. It was getting dark, and we had no luck getting the car back on the road. We were forced to walk three miles, maybe more, on a deserted dirt road until we reached the highway to hitch a ride.

I decided maybe the hills of Rancho California were not one of my favorite spots anymore.

Chapter 19

1928 Model A

Obtaining this vintage beauty was quite a production.

POP AND I DECIDED WE should have a joint hobby when we weren't going hunting. That made me feel good. I always thought we had a special relationship, although it was mostly unspoken.

As luck would have it, I was dating a looked named Terri. Her father owned the local drugstore. One afternoon over a chocolate milkshake at the fountain, I told her that my Pop and I were looking for a new hobby. She had an interesting suggestion.

"My father knows this old lady who owns an old Model A Ford that's just sitting in her garage." I got excited because it sounded like the perfect father-son project—restoring an old car.

(As I was to learn, the lady's husband had died more than a decade ago, and the car hadn't been driven since. She had a number of opportunities to sell the car but apparently didn't need the money, and the memories were important).

Terri took me home to meet her father. We had a short conversation about the matter. Since Terri was an only child, I could see her father liked the idea of a father-son hobby.

"My Pop doesn't say much," I joked. "Figured it might be a conversation starter. Since I don't know much about fixing cars, he'll have to say something."

Terri's father smiled. I could tell he liked my self-effacing sense of humor. Besides, we both knew, unlike a lot of typical teenage boys, I had always treated his daughter like a lady. He agreed to get my Pop and me an introduction to the lady.

I'm pretty sure Terri's father did some serious pre-selling because we were hardly in the front door when this sweet old lady said, "Father and son having a hobby together creates memories. John and I never had one." (I wasn't sure whether she was talking about a son or a hobby). She turned to me. "Young man, one day that car will give you a story for the grandchildren." (I still had no idea what the hell she was talking about. We were just buying an old car).

She offered to sell the car, sight unseen, at a price Pop's research suggested was around 10 percent of the fair market price. Pop agreed in a heartbeat. The man who lived to haggle and negotiate had already determined, no matter what shape the car was in, it was a good deal. The message that day? *When real opportunity knocks, don't be a grumpy old pig. Open the damn door and invite him in.*

Minutes later, the deal was consummated, and money changed hands. Damnedest thing, we still hadn't seen the car.

"Arthur, no matter what, with a little elbow grease and some imagination, we got you one hell of a car," proudly announced Pop on the way home. A few days later, Pop and I rented a car carrier and drove it to the lady's house to pick up our purchase. James drove over from his place to help.

"Out in the building next to the barn," pointed the lady. That's when James realized nobody had seen the car. He rolled his eyes. I shrugged.

It turned out there was no building next to the barn. Just a room with a three-foot-wide door that was connected to the barn.

We walked in. Wow! We were amazed. There sat a slant-window, limited-edition 1928 Model A in pristine condition. Obviously, the lady's husband knew something about restoration. The body repairs had been filled in with molten leading rather than that Bondo (cheap filler) stuff. The mohair seats looked like they had hardly been sat on, and the registration stickers and licenses were completely up to date. The lady had just kept renewing them. The only issues appeared to be a few flat tires, which was completely understandable, although it would make our job a little harder. James filled the tires with air. They bounced back to life. No leaks in sight.

I stated the obvious. "Should be no problem getting it on the trailer."

Pop laughed. "Agreed. That is, after we take down the whole side of the room to get her out."

James and I realized Pop was right. There was no way a four-foot-wide car could fit through a three-foot door. We looked around. There was a workbench and some tools. Pop insisted we take the wall apart board by board, so as "not to wreck the room."

Two hours later, we're covered in sweat and soot. "Get her on board," said Pop, pointing to our truck.

James and I obliged.

I couldn't wait to get our new toy home.

James got in his car. Pop shouted, "Where the hell do you think you're going?" James and I looked at each other.

Pop handed us each a hammer. "Let's get moving; we've got to get this wall back together before dark. Don't feel like driving all the way out here again."

~

During the next few years, Pop and I had great fun tinkering with the car and updating certain parts. But as time went by, Pop got busier and busier at work, and I had college and work.

I also discovered—post high school—that girls liked soft-spoken, self-effacing men but they weren't crazy about driving around in a 1928 Model A Ford in the year 1965.

Chapter 20

Pop's Secret Life

Pop kept lots of stuff to himself
if he didn't think there was a need to know.

I KNEW A LOT AND A LITTLE about my Pop.

He had three sisters and didn't finish high school. A few weeks before graduation, he decided to join the Coast Guard.

"I thought it was a pretty smart decision. The Army, Navy, and Marines get shot up. The Coast Guard just monitor the coastline," he explained later when I asked him why.

After the service, he tried a bunch of jobs to earn a living. The only one that stuck was the door-to-door Bible salesman job. But he wasn't crazy about it. "When you knock on the door, people think you want to steal their silverware."

He particularly liked to go fishing with his buddies near the village of San Felipe down the Baja Coast. Sometimes they'd be gone for a week.

He was also an avid gun collector. I remember he had quite a stash. But his pride and joy were a matching pair of German Lugers in a polished wooden box. Every so often, he'd say, "Arthur, someday these will be yours."

Somewhere along the line, he got a civil service job in California. He said working for the government was a steady paycheck with health benefits and a pension if you stuck it out. I never knew exactly what he did but, as time went by, we seemed to live better and better. All we knew for sure was that he had achieved a GS 14 grade, which for someone age 40 was high up the government totem pole.

I don't think Mom knew much more either. One evening, after James badgered him to death, POP cryptically mentioned something about overseeing supplies going to Vietnam. We tried to pump him for more information, but all he would say was, "Boys, nothing you need to know anything about."

~

Pop never had an office at home.

But every once and a while, the phone would ring, sometimes at the most peculiar hours, and Pop would ask my James and me if we'd like to visit his office at Norton Air Force Base. We always said yes because it was great fun. Norton had jet hangars the size of three football fields. His office was in the corner of one of the hangars. We were never allowed to enter his office; he'd simply say, "Gotta take care of a few things, so keep yourself busy." That was our signal to look at the sleek planes and hang out talking to some of his staff. They always gave us bottles of Coke, and one time, the staff let us look in the cockpit. Man, I never saw so many dials and gauges!

Every so often, Pop would announce he had to fly overseas for a week or two on business. He carried an attaché case with a combination lock and a small soft satchel with some clothes and toiletries, but not much else.

Mom seemed to know when the trip was coming up. But I don't think she knew much more than that. And, if she did, she never said anything to anybody.

~

Pop was strong as an ox.

I don't think in 23 years of work he took one sick day.

But he did suffer from the occasional migraine. One night the pain was so bad, he asked us to take him to the emergency room.

They took some information and then examined him. The nurses and doctors started pointing to his chart and then huddled out of earshot.

We were waiting and waiting by his bed in the emergency room. He was trying to be stoic, but I could tell he was in a lot of pain. Finally, I spoke. "Doc, my Pop is really hurting. Can't you give him something?"

The doctor shook his head no. "Sorry, we have to wait for official clearance."

"Clearance?"

"Your Pop has a top-secret clearance. Can't be too careful."

That's how James, Mom, and I learned Pop did something important for our country. It was like he had a whole other life.

I believe everybody has a secret they've never told anybody. I just don't know if that's good or bad.

Chapter 21

Hawkeye

I loved duck hunting.
Got me two big Canadian Honkers. Good eating.

ONE NEW YEAR'S EVE, my best friend and
hunting buddy, Jim Thomas, and I made a deal with our
wives. They rwanted to go to a big neighborhood New
Year's party. And, we wanted to go huntin first thing in
the morning. So we cut a deal We would escort them to
the party if they figured out how to get home. They
agreed. Jim and I kissed the girls at the stroke of
midnight then went off to hunt. (Never asked exactly
how they got home).

Jim had convinced me to borrow a boat and drive it
to the party since I owned a truck with a hitch and
managed to talk one of my Pop's friends into lending me
his aluminum 12-footer, complete with a powerful
outboard motor.

The night of the party arrived. I was straining to pack
the boat and lift it onto the hitch when Jim pulled into
the driveway and honked the horn for my wife to join
them. As he pulled away, he smiled, "Arthur, no worries;

I'll make sure the girls get to the party. Just don't forget any of the stuff." (I still wonder about how I got suckered into that deal, but Jim was such a sweet talker. He could pick your pocket and convince you to say thank you for the privilege.

Anyway, the party was a kick! It was a German theme with lots of beer and polkas. As agreed, about 1 a.m., Jim and I left the party to go hunting on the south end of the Salton Sea (a big lake on the outskirts of the Southern California desert) because we heard the "ducks were a flyin'."

By 3 a.m. we decided to bed down at the tip of a canal. The sound of the water gently rushing by created the sound of relaxation. Two hours later, I struggled to rise and began prepping for an early morning hunt. It finally dawned on me I was working solo. Jim had sat his butt at the rear of the boat, yawning and stretching.

"Hey buddy," I called out sarcastically, "I'm delighted to load all the decoys, the shotguns, the ammo, the supplies, and the water gear, while you map our course on the canal (it was about 8 feet wide)."

Jim got the point. He started looking around. "Arthur, what the hell happened to the motor?"

"What do you mean?"

"I mean there isn't one."

I was not about to admit I forgot the damn thing, so I said, "Ahhh, I decided we didn't need one. Makes the hunting more challenging."

He thought I was out of my mind.

"Here's the plan," I said. "The canal's flowing pretty good. All we gotta do is put the boat in the water and hop in; the current will take us down to the pond area where we can set up our duck blind."

"Are you crazy or just stupid?" replied Jim.

"What do you mean?"

"How do you propose we get back upstream?" asked Jim.

"Not a problem," I said reassuringly. "Thought about that. When we're finished, we'll just get a tow from one of the other hunters. No different than hitching a ride along the road."

(In retrospect, I should have known better. *If something sounds stupid, it probably is stupid*).

We debated the issue for a few minutes. Jim was getting hot under the collar. Finally, after some more whining and complaining, he reluctantly agreed to my "plan."

That's when *it* really hit the fan.

As we pushed the boat loaded with gear into the canal, I noticed the current was surprisingly strong. Maybe 10 miles an hour. At that point, even I was a little skeptical, but we had no choice—either jump in the boat or lose everything. Suddenly, we were hauling ass down the canal. Big time. Jim put his oar in the water to bring some direction to our flying ship. The damn thing snapped in half.

"What kind of dry rotted crap was that?" he glared.

"Buddy," I said, "don't lose your cool. I still got my oar."

I put my oar in the water. In a matter of seconds, I'm holding a splintered stub. I don't remember exactly what Jim said, but there were a lot of swear words and something about the tenuous nature of our future relationship.

As we whizzed along, I noticed there was a lot of thick brush on the right side of the boat. I reached out and attempted to hold on for dear life. My feet slid out from under me. I was stuck under the seat. Jim grabbed the rope attached to the front of the boat and jumped toward the bushes on the side of the canal to slow us down. He got badly scratched in the process. Somehow, we managed to steer the boat onto a path in the middle of some thick brush. We came to a screeching halt. I was lying on my back laughing like crazy.

Jim wasn't laughing, "Okay, genius, now we've got to get out of here. So, grab the damn rope and start pulling. I'll push from behind."

The boat seemed to weigh a ton as we dragged it along. Jim would have left the damn thing right there. He just wanted to go home. Suddenly, we heard some hunters coming down the path. "We're in luck; maybe these guys can help us."

I looked behind me. Jim had disappeared into the bushes. He didn't want to be embarrassed.

I figured I'll make like I was struggling, so they'd volunteer to help, and all would end well. To my surprise, the hunters watched me struggle for a few moments then burst into laughter. "Ever think of putting a motor on the boat and letting the water do the work?"

One of them looked at the sky and said, "Should be a heavy rain in a month or two. Just keep pulling." Then they walked away.

Somehow, we got the boat back to the car. We were a disgusting mass of perspiration.

Jim said nothing, making the long uncomfortable trip feel like forever.

~

Used to love to hunt. Pop had just put a new scope on one of his guns, and I had convinced him to lend it to me for the day.

Jim and I headed deep into the woods; we found an area where we could test our guns, check the calibrations, etc. Everything seemed fine, but I had missed the fact that Pop put the scope where he liked it—far back on the rifle.

Suddenly a hawk flew by. Like an idiot, I lifted my rifle up and began shooting in such a way that my right eye took the entire force of the recoil. The scope cut a half-circle above my right eye, and the blood started gushing down to my waist. Jim and my buddies howled. We stopped the bleeding just long enough to get me back to my house, so Mom could take me to the hospital and get me stitched up.

Along the way, I recall thinking *firing a gun without knowing exactly what to expect is a lot like marrying the wrong woman.*

After a visit to the emergency room, I was sore and embarrassed, but more determined than ever to nail that damn hawk. So, I headed back to the hunting area to find my buddies. Jim took one look and started howling. "Hey Hawkeye, lookin' good!" They handed me a mirror. I had a big circular black and blue mark around my entire eye. To make matters worse, the bruise didn't disappear for almost a month which gave the boys plenty of time for yuks around the girls.

It's almost forty years later, but whenever I talk to Jim on the phone, he still greets me the same way, "So, Hawkeye, how are you doing today?"

Part Two

Peaks and Valleys

Chapter 22

Big Art Goes Off-Road

Big Art loved souped up cars and powerful motorbikes.

POP LOVED OFF-ROAD motor biking.

He said it cleared his head. He even stored two bikes (and a jeep) at the air base. I think he figured that would make it impossible for James or me to go for an unauthorized spin. He was right about that!

~

One evening Pop was late for dinner, and he hadn't called. That was unusual. All we knew was that Pop and his buddy Jake had decided to check out some new hunting spot in the canyons after work.

It was now 8 p.m. The doorbell rang. The sheriff stood there, hat in hand. "Mrs. Mercado, there's no easy way to say this. Your husband is dead."

We were stunned. The invincible bull dead at 41!

"How did it happen?" asked Mom calmly.

"Not sure Ma'am. He and his buddy were biking in some steep, remote canyon. Guess they had trouble getting back out. Your husband and his buddy started pulling their bike up the hill. He suffered a massive heart attack. His buddy radioed for a helicopter. But by the time it arrived, he was gone."

Medical science knew a lot less about heart attacks back then, so the assumption was that he must have had an undiagnosed arterial block. I wouldn't be surprised if Pop had experienced some earlier signs but completely ignored them.

As I learned some time later, like father, like son.

~

That was that. Almost.

It turns out that Pop had died seven hours prior, at 1 p.m., not more than ten miles from our home. But, because of his top-secret government clearance, his death could not officially be declared until the FBI had searched his body and swept his office.

A few days later, we went to get his personal belongings. I remember a few things quite vividly. We were still not allowed to enter his office. There were two boxes of personal belongings on the landing area. A man introduced himself as Pop's boss. He said he was sorry that he had to be so impersonal, but that was policy "in these matters." The man explained that other than a book of military codes, there was nothing of consequence on Pop's body when he was found.

The other thing I remember was that while we waited outside Pop's office for his personal belongings, literally hundreds of people that worked for him stopped by to pay their respects.

The consensus? He was the toughest, fairest, and most generous boss, they ever had. *"His integrity was never for sale,"* as one person put it.

~

Big Art's funeral was at a small church in Yucaipa. It held about 300 people. There was an overflow of about another 100 or so folks who also paid their respects.

Mom was stunned but grateful that so many people cared about him.

Pop was also a 32^(ND) Degree Mason, so the clan had a grand Masonic service at his gravesite after the funeral. A representative flew in from Alabama, where he had first joined some 23 years prior. We were sad but proud.

That day, I promised Pop I'd follow his example on that integrity thing. It's 38 years later, and I haven't broken my word yet.

I assume he knows.

~

Over the years, I've thought about my Pop's untimely death many times. To be honest, sometimes I've even got mad with God. There are so many people in this world who just drift through. They don't do anything, and they don't leave anything. It's taken me a lot of years, but I think I've finally figured it out the meaning of Pop's life. By taking him early, God was telling me, *"Arthur, make every day of your life count. Let people know you've been here. Leave your legacy, not by what you say, or you accomplish in material terms, but by your actions."*

Chapter 23
Raising Mindy

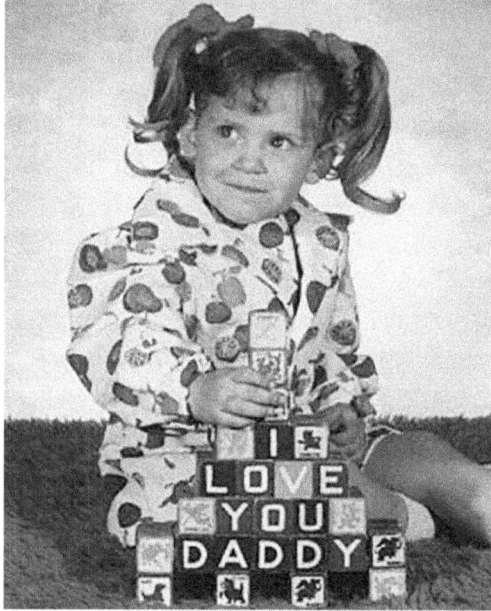

Mindy, age 3, had no idea of the turmoil surrounding her.

MY FIRST MARRIAGE TO MINDY'S mom, Lynn, didn't go so well.

Let's just say there was enough blame to go around. She didn't do the right things as a wife, and in those days, I probably wasn't the easiest person to live with. In fact, if I were her, I probably would have left me!

In the end, however, I'd have to say I did more things right than wrong because it took the judge only about twenty minutes to award me full custody of Mindy when she was four. In those days, that was quite a legal accomplishment for the father to receive full custody. You had to be beyond squeaky clean. The courts were like bloodhounds. A simple speeding ticket could invalidate your motion! (I know you're wondering why, but sometimes it's better just to move on. It was a long time ago).

Anyway, there we were. My beautiful baby daughter and her single working father. Alone. With no one to depend on but ourselves.

It occurred to me straight away; I didn't want to be like a lot of other fathers. Sure, I wanted discipline and order, but I vowed to never raise my voice or my hand to Mindy. I would set reasonable ground rules, she'd know I meant them, and that would be that. I believed, and still do, if a child blatantly disobeys a parent the first time, it's the parent's fault. Either they weren't clear about the rules or didn't register the severity of the consequences. If a child disobeys a second time, it's a different matter.

I never once got to "a second time" with Mindy. In fact, I can't even remember a first time of consequence.

~

I remember our first discussion of the rules like it was yesterday.

About two months after I had gained custody, Mindy was salivating over the candy sitting in a three-tier antique serving dish that sat on a circular table in the corner of the living room. Generally, it was filled with the kind of stuff my sweet tooth loved but would be quite messy in the hands of children or not consistent with their taste buds. Things like chocolate-covered, liquid-filled cherries.

I said, "Mindy, do you want some candy?"

"Yes, Poppy," she replied sweetly.

"Tell you what, that dish and that candy in it are off limits." I took out another dish and placed it on the table. "Let's make this dish Mindy's candy dish. Every week I'll put a certain amount of candy in the dish. Enough for you to enjoy, but not so much to spoil your appetite or do bad things to your teeth...Plus, there'll be little chance of you accidentally breaking one of Poppy's favorite dishes in the whole world."

Mindy smiled and nodded.

I continued. "If you decide to eat all the candy before the week is out, you can't touch the candy in the other dish. You must wait until it's time to refill your dish. Do you understand?"

Mindy said, "Yes, Poppy." She was true to her word. She never even tried to eat a piece of candy out of the antique dish.

~

The key word in our relationship has always been "respect."

When Mindy was ten, there were ground rules that were appropriate for a ten-year-old. She had to keep her dresser neat and organized. One time I checked the room, and it was a mess. I took all her clothes out of the drawers and asked her to organize them properly, as we had agreed. She never let that happen again.

As she got older, the ground rules changed. I told her it was her job to keep her room and our house orderly. In return, I would never enter her room without permission. She kept her end of the bargain, and I never broke my rule once.

~

We also established mutual ground rules. If she went out with a friend or on a date, we would agree what time she would be home. If she wasn't going to fulfill our agreement, she would call and explain why. I told her I loved her, and I didn't want to worry. Until she was 18, she only missed once. She and her girlfriend Joanne fell asleep at Joanne's house watching television in the family room. I called 60 minutes after curfew, and Joanne's Mom had to wake Mindy up to put her on the telephone.

But, as I said, the ground rules were mutual. If I was going out on a date or whatever, Mindy knew exactly what time to expect my return. I never missed my curfew once. (Sometimes, the excuse served me well when the date was less than interesting).

On her 18th birthday, we went out to dinner to celebrate. I again told her I loved her and that she was now a woman. She smiled and asked, "Does that mean my curfew is extended?"

My response? "Mindy, you're now an adult. There is no longer a curfew. But as long as you live with me, I'd appreciate knowing what time you plan to come home."

That daughter makes me so proud. She was, and still is, so respectful; there were rarely any surprises.

That doesn't mean we didn't have our little disagreements. I remember Mindy getting so mad about something I said (I still don't remember what it was) that she took every personal item I ever bought her—jewelry, rings, dresses, the works and put them to one side of her room for weeks. She wouldn't touch them.

Goes to show you, don't cross a woman unless you want hell to pay!

~

There was one other value I stressed…independence.

My feeling is *you should love your fellow man without reservation, but you should be dependent on no one for nothing.* Makes life a lot less complicated.

Over the years, I taught Mindy how to fix cars, do plumbing, electrical, and general repairs. Today, she owns and uses an extensive collection of power tools. Along the way, she also taught herself how to crochet, sew, and cook.

I remember when she was about ten I taught her about shopping for value. I'd make out the grocery list and then estimate the cost of the groceries and put the money on the table. "That is our money," I would say, "Now, if you find coupons in the newspapers and the mail that reduces the bill, that money is yours." It wasn't long before she was making twenty cents on every dollar spent.

Today, Mindy's got four kids, and she's still one of the best coupon clippers I've ever seen.

~

When Mindy was in junior high she taught me about the benefits of independence. I was driving a white two-seat Corvette. One day, we decided the cupboard was almost bare, and we needed to go grocery shopping. We reviewed what we needed and made a proper list.

In the supermarket, we had a lot of fun comparison shopping and taking full benefit of on-sale items and store specials. Mindy saved us a bundle, so we bought for the moment and for a rainy day. When we returned to the car with the cart brimming over, we realized we had so much stuff there wasn't enough room for me, Mindy and all the groceries.

I said, "I'll bring the groceries home and come right back." She was a little apprehensive. But I told her, "I won't be long."

As I pulled away, she looked like a frightened rabbit. By the time I returned about 15 minutes later, she was sitting on a milk crate talking to some ladies. They were all smiling and laughing. "Your daughter has quite a sense of humor," winked one lady. "She was just telling us her Poppy had to drive the groceries home."

~

I may be on the way to becoming a stubborn old fart, but I believe *if more parents and their children showed mutual respect, the need to take stern disciplinary actions would be few and far between.* I also believe the adage, "Spare the rod and spoil the child" is a bunch of hooey.

Chapter 24

Claims Adjuster

Introverted, shy me discovers I'm a natural salesman...
among other things

AFTER A FEW YEARS OF RAISING Mindy by myself, I realized the single-parent thing was like a full-time job, especially if you wanted to do it right.

Speaking of jobs, I was now the Director of Quality Control for a medical respirator company called the Bird Corporation, located in Palm Springs about a 40-mile commute from our home in Banning.

I worked there about 7½ years and had done everything from managing the production department to establishing corporate quality controls to building product prototypes.

One day, the owner, Dr. Bird (Ph.D.), approached me. "Arthur, I've got this idea for a flow respirator that can accommodate a wide range of patients from infants to adults. (At that time, respirators were designed with flow volumes for a specific patient class, i.e., average adults, infants, etc.). He told me he wanted me to finish the design, build test equipment, and prepare the successful prototypes for production, as well as write the assembly and test procedure manuals.

But that was only the half of it. He said when all this was done, he was planning to move the company to Sand Point, Idaho, where he had just purchased 200 acres not far from a magnificent lake filled with fish and surrounded by mountains. He wanted me to run the manufacturing department.

I took a trip to visit the area. The site was beautiful, the town and surrounding area seemed perfect to raise Mindy. There were also "other perks." I would have a condo on the lake, a company car, and the use of a company boat. Plus, the good Doctor said I could use one of the company planes to go back down to visit friends and take some R&R whenever I wanted. I was jacked.

Six months later, I completed the prototypes and procedure manuals. Another six months passed, and I was still in Palm Springs, traveling all over the place visiting installation sites. I hinted. Nothing. It was clear I'd been used and he was not going to keep his word. It was time to look for another job.

~

I decided to stop by the office of my buddy Jim "Hawkeye" Thomas who was making a nice living selling insurance for the AAA. The receptionist said, "Jim's working out of his house today, scheduling appointments, and seeing prospects."

I said to myself, I've gotta get a job like Jim. Something that would allow me to be home with Mindy during the day and still make a good living. Next thing I know, Jim set up an interview with his manager. The guy seemed to like me, but there was a glitch—there wasn't an opening in the entire Palm Springs area. He did me a favor and called around. It turned out there was a sales opening in the Pomona office, just south of Los Angeles. I told Mindy we're moving. She seemed happy that we were getting out of the stifling summer heat.

~

AAA was and still is a first-class operation. They wanted me to complete a three-week training course before I started talking to customers. The training facility was on Figueroa Street in downtown L.A. It wasn't a great neighborhood, but I had a room at the Hilton, which was a first-class property, so I figured I could grin and bear it.

I decided to buy a new business wardrobe, sort of a break from the past. I bought a few new suits, ties, shoes and shirts, but I kept my watches, chains, and other accessories. Since I only owned an open-air Jeep at the time, I borrowed my ex-wife Linda's AMC (American Motor Company) yellow Gremlin, packed my belongings, and headed to the City. By the way, that Gremlin was brand spanking new but had to be the ugliest car I ever drove!

"One little problem," said the office manager. "You start bright and early Monday morning."

"Yup," I smiled.

"Turned out the Hilton was booked solid Sunday night, so we put you up at the nearby Vagabond. Okay?" I figured no big deal. One night without the comfort of Hilton security was not going to kill me.

I arrived in the dark. The place was an absolute dump! But, I figured what the hell. I had some dinner at Denny's across the street, and headed to bed. I tucked my good watch and all my other jewelry in a clothes bag in the closet. There was a knock on the door. I was right near the vending machines, so I figured somebody was looking for change. I opened the door, and there was this long-haired chick staring at me. Behind her was this big dude with a gun pointed at my face. Next thing I know, I'm hogtied on the floor, and this guy was smashing me in the face with his gun. Once, twice, three times. Maybe four. I was bleeding but still pretty defiant. I told him, "You better not let me loose because I'll kill you with my bare hands."

"Where's the jewelry?" he said, as he ransacked the closet. I told him it was in the trunk of the car.

Next thing I know, they've taken my entire wardrobe —absolutely everything—grabbed the keys to the Gremlin and sped off. I struggled to get free. No luck. Somehow, I crawled to the phone. The guy had cut the cord. I heard somebody cursing at the vending machine. I yelled for help. Turned out it was the manager. The machine had swallowed his quarter. He freed me and called the cops. They showed up two hours later!

The cop said, "Sir, you're damn lucky."

I thought to myself, *where they hell have you been? On a coffee break?*

He continued. "Just came from another crime scene. A couple with the same MO robbed a guy and shot him right in the face."

~

Things got better after that.

I absorbed the training like a sponge. Mostly common sense and a few insurance tests. I came out of the box smoking. I was motivated to succeed for me and Mindy, and to show Dr. Bird what he had lost. It's not long before I noticed my soft-sell sales tactics worked like crazy. And not long after that, I'm selling as much insurance as anybody in the office and having the flexibility to tend to my parental responsibilities.

~

I noticed something else. I'm a single, available male, in my early 30's, and the office was populated by a slew of attractive women. The girls thought I was a nice guy, a caring single parent and all. One thing led to another. I exchanged a few pleasantries, maybe a flirt or two. Next thing I knew, there were notes in my mail box. The prettiest girl in the office had the most intriguing note. "Please meet me at the park down the street after work. I have something important to tell you."

I discreetly dropped a note in her box with a day and time. "Now what did you want to tell me?" I asked naively sitting on the park bench.

She told me she just wanted to see what it was like to kiss me. I think I said, "Oh," and walked away.

~

I was probably the most sought-after, unmarried guy in the office with every woman but one...the Senior Claims Adjuster, Rosie.

Rosie was cute as a button. No taller than 5-1 or 2, olive-toned Mexican with dark brown eyes, straight long hair, and a perfectly proportioned figure. Lots of guys in the office tried to get to first base with no success. I decided to be a little more subtle. I realized she had to walk by the sales office whenever she took a break in the employee dining area. I decided to start taking my break when Rosie took her break. At first, I just made small talk. She quickly realized our "chance meetings" were not a coincidence.

I finally decided to ask her out on a date. She explained she never dated men in the office. Too complicated. She lived with her mother and father because she had experienced an unpleasant divorce.

I stayed cool. No rush. I was confident she'd eventually wear down. We shared coffee, donuts, newspapers, and jokes. Next thing I know, it was two years later. Life was good. I was the top salesmen in the office. I was making good money, had parenting Mindy down to a science, and dated all the available women in the office but one—Rosie.

I decided it was time to change my approach strategy. In my first two years as an AAA insurance salesmen, I had become a master at using little buy-ins before going for the big close.

I suggested coffee after work. I knew what Rosie's answer was going to be, but I had a plan. She expressed reluctance. There was this excuse and that excuse. But she didn't flat-out say no. That's when I knew I had her. *When a woman doesn't say no, she means yes.*

One Friday, I was standing by her desk. I smiled. "How about we just go out for breakfast?" I mean jeez, that's a day date. How innocent can you get?" She looked directly into my eyes, then nodded. That Saturday morning, I picked her up at 6 a.m. sharp in my cool, classy, custom copper-colored Porsche with dark copper pin-striping.

"I'm thinking breakfast in Santa Barbara." She was a bit taken by my ingenuity. It was quite a first date. Just before we reached Santa Barbara, I spotted a polo game. Lots of fancy cars in the lot. We pulled in and made like part of the crowd. Thank goodness nobody asked us the score or stuff like that. The rest of the day was spent walking college campuses, listening to music in a park gazebo, walking the beach, and stopping for lunch. By dinner time, we were tired and a little grubby looking. I had to bribe a waiter to let us into an upscale restaurant. We sat in the corner. By the time I dropped her back off at her mother's house it was midnight. So much for the daytime date!

Things progressed quickly after that. I began spending serious money on her. She loved fresh roses, but not ordinary red ones. She preferred pinks, yellows, and other pastels. Before long, I was going to the florist every week to pick out the freshest dozen. I had the process down to a science. I'd get there just before the official opening on Monday. The shopkeeper would open the door special for me, so I could always get first choice.

Then there was the jewelry. Rings, necklaces, chains, and bracelets. She had to have more bling than any woman I had ever met. Heck, she was happy, and I was in the state of a euphoria. Or, so I thought. Mindy didn't say much, and, shame on me; I never thought to ask her about how she felt about our relationship. In any event, Rosie and I got married. Before long, I sold the Porsche to help buy a house.

Two problems quickly surfaced. I had developed a gambling problem, and the bills are backing up. I asked for help. My pleas fell on deaf ears. Rosie told me it was my problem to fix. That wasn't the answer I wanted, but, in retrospect, I guess she was right.

The other problem was the Mindy-Rosie relationship. One day the school called to tell me she was crying in school. We sat down and talked. Reluctantly, she told me that she'd been treated rudely by Rosie. Lots of little things. Petty jealousies. I asked why she hadn't said anything before. The answer broke my heart, "Poppy, I wanted you to be happy." *I realized I had put my desires ahead of my daughter's emotional well-being.* I never did that before, and I've never done it since.

In a matter of weeks, I unraveled the marriage, leaving with nothing but Mindy and our personal belongings. I also cleaned up my gambling act and haven't missed one payment on one bill in twenty years.

This experience also taught me something else. *The right woman completes your life.* It would take a while, but once I found Susan, it was game, set, match. Forever and ever.

Chapter 25

Ernestine Passes

Pop at 41, James at 36, and Mom at 57.
The Mercado's sure knew how to love 'em and leave 'em.

MOM HAD BEEN SICK on and off for quite some time. We knew something was wrong, but Mom and Pop never wanted to talk about it in front of us kids.

This time was different. Mom complained of severe headaches openly, so we knew they had to be terrible because she rarely complained. Pop took her to the doctor. She was diagnosed with ovarian cancer. (Two of my uncles had just died from cancer; the agony they endured and their pain-ridden faces were fresh in my mind).

Next thing I know, Mom completed a series of tests at the hospital, and the doctor provided Mom and Pop with a somber diagnosis. I was about ten at the time, so the details are a bit hazy. But I remember the doctor told Mom and Pop that cobalt radiation treatments were the ticket. Publically, Pop was skeptical since, at that time, the treatment was rather primitive, painful and unproven.

Privately, I assume Mom and Pop discussed the potential side effects, and, like always, she won the debate. Things were never the same after Mom's treatments began. Pop would come home from work, have dinner with my brother and me, and then we'd all go to visit Mom at the hospital.

She got radiation poisoning from the first round of treatments. She also became massively dehydrated, followed by bouts of pain. Her frail little body looked like a sack of bones. I can still see her crying and screaming in that hospital room. I didn't understand all that was going on at the time, except that she had received too much radiation and suffered massively because of the miscalculation.

By Thanksgiving, Ernestine Mae was weak but recovering. Most importantly, with the proper dosage, she was beginning to tolerate the treatments better. She insisted the family's traditional Thanksgiving dinner must go on. I helped out by cooking my first turkey. It was damn good.

But my Mother was to be sick for the rest of her life. After Pop died, I became the family's "go-to guy." Mom knew I was always there for her. There were so many ailments, so many late-night trips to the emergency room. But I loved her like crazy. It was never a chore. Whenever she summoned, I would hustle over to the house, rush her to the hospital, stay there all night by her side, and then go to work the next morning.

~

Eventually, I had Mom move in with me so I could take better care of her. Mindy loved having her grandmother living with her, and so did I. In some ways, it was like growing up all over again. There were all the family stories of all the good times.

The years passed. Mom was now very frail and continuously tired, but she insisted she wanted to live in New Orleans with her mother and sister. I sensed she knew the end was near. We debated the wisdom of the request. Like always, Mom won.

Shortly after that, I attached a U-Haul trailer to the back of my pick-up truck, and filled it with her furniture. I began the long journey to New Orleans alone in the truck. Mom, God bless her, was not far behind driving her brand new 1976 light blue Mercury sedan (she insisted she needed that car).

A few months later, Mom was on the phone sobbing. She was in pain and missed her doctors. I knew I had to bring her back. I flew back to New Orleans. She looked dreadful. I got another trailer, attached her Mercury to it, and packed all her furniture, including a few large pieces that almost gave me a hernia. This time, there was no argument about her driving back, she was simply too weak.

Instead, I arranged a private railroad car for the two-day trip because I wanted her to be as comfortable as possible. I also I found the porter who would be servicing mom's compartment, gave him half of all the money I had and told him to "spoil my mom in every way possible." *(I've always believed money is for spending. Especially when it's for a good cause).*

I then drove 30 straight hours back to California to beat the train. When I got there, I again unloaded all of Mom's belongings in my house. There was no chance she was ever going to live alone again. When Mom got to the house, I proudly introduced her to her furnished and decorated room. She didn't say much, except that she loved me, was proud of me, and knew I would always be there for her. I was sad, but she made me feel super special.

~

Mindy and I did our best to make Mom comfortable. It was during this difficult period that Mindy and Mom bonded beyond belief. One night she complained of severe pains in her side. We had her admitted to Loma Linda Hospital. The doctors found a lump on her kidney.

She underwent surgery almost immediately to reduce the possibility of the cancer metastasizing elsewhere. I stayed at the hospital until she was out of surgery. To everyone's surprise, the surgery went better than expected She had little postsurgical discomfort. Plus, the doctors said that they removed all the cancerous tissue, and she was going to be okay. I remember it was early in the day, so I figured I'd go to work. I kissed her goodbye on the cheek. She smiled. "Go, I'll be fine."

She would call me at work to say hello. I came and visited her at the hospital every day. Sometimes, I'd just sit there and hold her hand. She said she could feel my love and it gave her strength. I'm not sure I ever told her how important that made me feel. Don't know why.

The hospital staff just loved mom's moxie, her sweetness and the fact that she rarely complained despite the frequent bouts of pain. They nicknamed her "Tiny."

She was scheduled to come home in a few days when I got the strangest call. She was begging me to come quick. She said someone or something was trying to get her. She said whatever it was, was cutting a hole in the wall to get her. She screamed, "Somebody help me. They are coming after me. They're coming after me." I told her I'd be right over. I never drove so fast. I was there in less than 30 minutes.

When I arrived, the room was full of doctors and nurses. They asked who I was. I told them I was her son, and that she had just called me. They said Mom had died of a heart attack minutes ago, and they had failed at all attempts to bring her back.

To this day, I regret not staying in that room with her. I still feel I could have held her hand, given her strength, and talked her through whatever was happening.

Only-if-I-had guilt can last a lifetime, so make certain you don't incorrectly believe it was your fault.

~

Mom's funeral was uneventful, compared to Pop's. There wasn't much family left, and she had been sick so long that she didn't have a lot of friends outside the family.

Of course, the Mercado family seems to have a flair for the dramatic. During the week of Mom's funeral, my other grandmother died.

Chapter 26

Den Mother

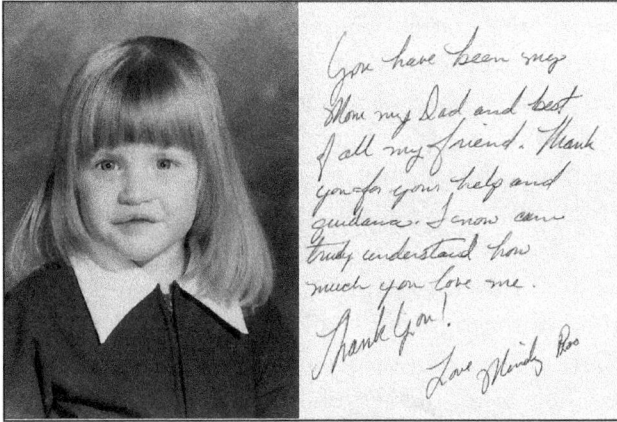

My little munchkin got an A+ on her story about me.

THE PHONE RANG. A lady from Mindy's school introduced herself as the head of the PTA and asked for "Mrs. Mercado."

Mindy's was now in the fourth grade, and I'd been a single parent for almost seven years. We had moved from one part of town to another, which caused her to transfer from a private to a public school, and frankly, she had been struggling despite her obvious intelligence.

Consequently, I assumed the call had something to do with her grades.

I responded, "I'm Mr. Mercado. What can I do for you?"

Obviously, I wasn't clear. The lady insisted it was a matter for Mrs. Mercado, at which point I explained, "I'm also Mrs. Mercado."

She said, "Oh, my," then paused.

I took the bull by the horns. "What seems to be the problem?"

"Somebody signed up Mrs. Mercado to be a room mother. I was just calling to explain what was expected when the next event was, and so on."

I asked the lady to wait a minute while I got to the bottom of the matter. The fact was, I knew. To Mindy, I had always been her Mom, Pop, and her best friend. I walked over to the stairs and called upstairs. "Marinda, come down here." (She knew when I called her Marinda I was mad, which was rare).

"Marinda, there's a lady on the phone, telling me Mrs. Mercado signed up to be a room mother. Did you forge my name?" I tried to express stern displeasure. I had all I could do not to bust out laughing.

Now it was her turn to try to appear serious. She bowed her head. "Guess I did," she replied, at which point we both broke out laughing.

I ask the PTA president what was involved. She said the mothers were meeting on the following Friday to discuss plans for a bake sale. I told her, "Count me in; I'll be there." What the hell, I was a good cook, and it was for a good cause.

~

Mom's meeting day arrived.

I got there a little late from the office. I walked in. There were 25 women and me. I sat down at a desk in the rear of this big room. The 50 eyes followed my every move. I tried to be cool. I smiled and just listened. The PTA president attempted to explain the event details. Nobody noticed they were all still staring at me. I was certain they wanted me out of there. Finally, the PTA president realized what was going on.

"Ladies," she said, "let me make something clear. *Mrs.* Mercado is not going away. She volunteered just like the rest of you."

And that was that.

We moved on to the agenda. The idea was to celebrate the kids' school year with a giant bake-off party. Different moms volunteered to bake brownies and cookies, make the punch. I volunteered to make the cupcakes. The women in the room smiled. I was now officially one of the girls!

Heck, I figured, how hard could it be to make three or four dozen cupcakes? You just whip up the batter, pour it into those little paper holders, and stick them in the oven, and from time-to-time check them with a toothpick. If the toothpick slides out clean, they're done. (Mom taught me that trick when I was about ten and was learning to cook myself).

Besides, I loved sweets. When we finished, I figured there would be a few extra ones for me.

Next day, I explained the story to a few buddies at the office. Everybody had a good yuck. That night before I left for my kitchen, I noticed that somebody had placed a big red apron on my desk. Next to it sat a mixing bowl and a wooden spoon. There was a small gift card. It read "for Mrs. Mercado."

~

Dinner was done. It was baking time.

Mindy and I had a ball. I mixed the batter. She helped me put the stuff in the cupcake tins. When I poured too much, she had this little cloth and wiped the excess. The kitchen smelled great. Before long, the toothpicks were sliding out, and there were four dozen plus cupcakes cooling on the counter. Mindy insisted she decorate them all. She used cans of colored icing and a few jars of multi-colored sprinkles.

The job was done, and it was past her bedtime. "Poppy," she said, placing a small dish in front of me, "I saved these for us." There were five beautifully decorated cupcakes.

We sat, had milk, and ate the goodies. Damn, they tasted great!

I brought the cupcakes to the event the next day. The kids must have thought they tasted good. They were the first thing to go.

The cupcake caper taught me two things. First, Mindy was on her way to becoming a great cook. She still loves to bake. She makes the most fabulous, most yummy pumpkin pecan pie in the whole world.

The other thing I learned was that *being a male chef like James Beard wasn't homo.*

Chapter 27

Snake Charmer

I've always had a "hands-on" relationship with snakes.

I'VE ALWAYS MAINTAINED a healthy curiosity and respect for snakes. Now, I'm not talking any snakes; I'm talking about those

venomous California Rattlers—the Diamond Back, Timbers, and Sidewinders mostly. Some friends might even characterize me as a little peculiar in that respect. But snakes have taught me some valuable life lessons.

My brother James and I use to like to hunt in a place called Rattlesnake Canyon, Camp Angeles, in the mountains near Glendora. We had been hunting venison for the better part of the morning and were dead tired. We spotted a big stack of leaves. I suggested we relax a bit on our newfound mattresses as we map out the rest of the day's trail. I stretched out on one side of the pile; Bro did likewise on the other. Suddenly, a large rattlesnake tail —eight rattles as I recall—popped up through the leaves. I jumped out of my pants while James maintained a calm curiosity. We scratched away some leaves with our gun butts. "That's one big son of a bitch," said James, taking his Remington 7MM rifle and blowing the snake's head off.

"Where the hell did you learn to do that?" I asked.

"Saw it in a comic book," he laughed.

Then we buried the head, to make sure nobody could accidentally get stuck by one of those killer fangs.

James looked at his watch. "You hungry? Almost lunch time."

Next thing I know, we cut the sucker open, removed the vertebrae, sliced our friend into chunks, seasoned 'em with some salt and pepper, and skewered the pieces over a crackling hot fire...tasted pretty damn good!

That incident taught me another of life's little lessons. *When it comes to rattlesnakes, ask questions later!*

~

On another occasion, I was walking up my driveway after work. I had some friends coming over for drinks and cards. There was a big branch in the driveway, so I pushed it to the side with my foot so nobody would trip over it.

All of a sudden, the stick moved. I was looking directly at a head of a five-foot rattler. Calmly, I got my rake out of the garage, put the sucker in a big bucket, and called the Humane Society. Mindy thought I was crazy. (It wasn't the first or last time she thought that).

As time passed, I met so many rattlers in so many places, I damn near became a rattler scholar. Hell, I even developed Arthur's "rattlesnake philosophy," i.e., *if you spot a rattler, and he's not bothering you, just leave the damn thing alone.*

~

Another time I was boating on a lake near Paso Robles with my sister Lori, my three nephews, and Mindy. There was nothing but calm waters, rolling hills, and lush terrain as far as the eye could see. The weather was also spectacular—bright sun, blue skies, low humidity, and just enough breeze on the lake.

After circling a few nearby islands, Lori suggested we stop and have lunch. With three strong boys, I figured it would be a cinch to row to shallow water and have them pull us to dry land.

We found a nice spot under a tree. The entire lake was in front of us. The kids ate everything in sight.

Nephew Ricco suggested they explore. The brush didn't look particularly dense, so we agreed to let them go. The kids followed Ricco. Five minutes later Ricco was screaming at the top of his lungs, "Snake, snake!"

I thought the worst. Somebody got bit, or somebody was trapped. I grabbed my hunting knife and started running, hacking away branches as I went.

When I caught up with them, the kids were standing around a motionless snake. I recognized it immediately. It was one of those small, deadly sidewinders (about 24 inches long and thin as a magic marker). Fortunately, he was dead as a doornail. I started laughing.

"Kids, nothing to be frightened about." They relaxed and started laughing. I picked the damn thing up near its head; the eyes opened, and the fangs started hissing. I dropped the thing like a hot potato, grabbed a big rock, and started pounding the head until it was lifeless.

Everybody was screaming and wailing. I figured we might as well head back across the lake or turn the event into an educational experience. "Kids, there's nothing to be frightened about. Old mister snake is dead. Do you guys know snakes make good eating? They taste a lot like chicken. How about we roast him over a fire?"

The kids went "ugh," and Lori said something about me being crazy. I decided it was time for plan B.

My mind flashed back to three years earlier in Palm Springs. It was break time so I sat on the rear deck near my office and watched the private planes land and take off at the airport next store.

Om my short walk back, I noticed a board sitting on the ground. Figuring it would be just my luck to trip over the damn thing, I picked it up and tossed it in the dumpster. There on the ground in front of me was some fool snake that got crushed and suffocated. I picked the thing up and suddenly the damn thing started to squirm and hiss.

I dropped the sucker and started smashing it in the head with a board until I was certain it was dead.

Life's a lot like a barrel of snakes. Some people learn to keep away from trouble the first time out. Fools need to make the same mistake a few more times before they back away.

Chapter 28

My Brother Ernie

James was two years older than me.
I called him Ernie. Not sure why.

MY OLDER BROTHER JAMES suffered from migraine headaches most of his adult life.

At age 36, he finally agreed to have a battery of tests run and was admitted to the Queen of the Valley hospital. I decided to visit him after work. As the elevator door opened on his floor, there was James dressed in a suit and tie. I asked him where the hell he thought he was going.

"It's time to get out of here," he said.

"Ernie," I said (James was Jimmy to Mom, James to Pop and Ernie to me. It never made any sense, and I don't know how it started), it's my understanding the tests aren't finished."

We argued about the wisdom of him returning to his room. I noticed a few stares from the staff.

Reluctantly, he agreed. We started walking down the hall past this gorgeous nurse. She smiled but was all business.

"Your brother certainly has a mind of his own," she sighed.

"I'll get him back in bed."

She nodded. "Maybe you can talk some sense into him."

I smiled. "I doubt it."

She didn't laugh.

Ernie started to undress behind the curtain in his room. I heard the nurse returning.

I decided the entire situation could use a little levity. I climbed into Ernie's bed in my suit. He hid out of view. When the nurse arrived, we all cracked up. Mission accomplished!

I told Ernie, no matter what, he was taking the tests. I drove Mindy to Palm Springs to stay with a few friends for the weekend. "I'll call to check in once we're settled. I'll be back before the lab results arrive on Monday."

He smiled, "Later, bro."

I mumbled something dumb like "cool."

Little did I know those would be the last words we'd say to each other!

After Mindy had settled in with my friends, I got this funny feeling something was not right. I called the hospital. The nurse said, "Your brother has taken a turn for the worse. You better get back here."

I flew down the highway to the hospital. I got to his room around midnight. He was on life support. Ernie's wife, Sophia, stood motionless by his side.

"What the hell happened?" I asked.

"Nobody knows for sure," she said. "Your brother just slipped into a coma."

Suddenly, Ernie started to talk, clear as a bell, with his eyes closed.

"I can't reach the door."

"What door?" asked Sophia.

He slipped back into the coma. Ernie went in-and-out twice more. Each time he referred to the imaginary door he couldn't reach. I was pretty sure I knew the door Ernie was talking about. When we were growing up, Pop taught us colored doors were signs. Red meant death. Green meant life. Yellow meant you weren't sure.

Suddenly, Ernie asked what time it was. Sophia said 9 p.m. He asked, "Are you sure?" She said, "It's your watch, James. Your watch." My brother was always fascinated by watches. He had an extensive collection, and because he was an engineer, he seemed more obsessed than most about the precise time of day.

A split-second passed. Ernie responded, "I've gotta go." Then he slipped into a deep coma.

I took the doctor aside. "Your brother has an irreversible brain hemorrhage; there's nothing we can do. I'm sorry."

I told the doctor about the pact James and I made with each other a long time ago. *If the time came when there was no hope for one of us, the other would authorize the disconnection to avoid any undue suffering.*

There wasn't much else to say at that point. The doctor nodded.

"If you can get his wife out of the room, I'll disconnect your brother."

I explained the situation to Sophia with tears in my eyes. She understood. Ernie passed in a matter of minutes. He was just 36. I decided to stay with Sophia the entire night. In the morning, I searched his desk for relevant paperwork such as wills. In his desk drawer was a folder with everything we needed for his funeral arrangements and final requests. Obviously, he had a premonition.

~

It was noon the day of Ernie's' funeral. The phone rang. It was Cousin Dorothy from New Orleans. I figured she must have heard about my brother and was calling to offer condolences.

"I thought you'd want to be the first to know," she said. "My mom died yesterday."

Aunt Brown was only 47, so I was surprised and saddened.

"What happened?"

"She apparently had a massive heart attack in her sleep."

I said something about being very sorry and then asked: "How is Grandma Albie (Aunt Brown's mother) holding up?" I loved that lady so and was deeply concerned.

Dorothy's response "I'm not sure how to answer because Grandma's dead also. Best we can figure, Grandma Albie found Mom in bed and also had a massive heart attack. We never heard a sound from either incident. We had no idea what happened until we went looking for them to sit down for breakfast."

I was speechless. My mind flooded with bizarre, macabre thoughts. "Jesus, we're going to need two more holes."

When the dust settled that weekend, I asked God what was that all about. I never heard from him then or since.

But I do think about James almost every day. Sometimes, when I feel overwhelmed by my own problems, I give him a call, and we just talk.

One time he told me talking to someone you love in a moment of crisis makes everything right with the world. He was right.

Chapter 29

$500 Sport Coat

*My "cool" period. $500 sports jacket, burnt orange shirt,
cream colored slacks, and loud tie.*

ALWAYS BELIEVED MONEY WAS for spending.

I was fortunate enough to make a decent buck as an insurance salesman. Because I was a good salesman with a streak of honesty, it made some of the "quick buck" peers scratch their heads. Naturally, I shared the wealth with Mindy—nice dresses, hats, and stuff. Once she was a teenager, I began to spoil her with jewelry.

I also made sure I treated myself well. I loved sports car and dressing in nice clothes. I considered myself "fashion-aware." I even had my own account at a high-end men's shop in town. I figured whatever I didn't know about fashion; they could keep me current. Plus, they had a reputation for quality.

One day, I was casually browsing through the racks. I had just been told I won the annual top salesman award and that I would be receiving in front of my peers at our annual conference. I started looking through the men's sports coats. There it was. My dream jacket. It was so cool! (I thought). Cream colored with big bold brown squares. I tried it on. It fit like a glove.

John, my regular sales guy, said, "Arthur, that jacket has your name on it. It doesn't even need a stitch of alteration."

"How much?"

"It's expensive.'

"How much is expensive?"

"It's 100% pure linen. They didn't make many of them."

"How much?"

"Five hundred dollars."

"Holy Crap!" I'm flabbergasted. I'd never spent that much on a single piece of clothing in my life. But I loved it. "How about I put it on layaway."

"No problem."

I gave John $50. I figured the award program wasn't for another two months, so I had time to pay off the balance. But things happened. I got real busy at work, Mindy had a cold that won't quit, and I had a ton of home repair projects stacked up. I completely forgot about the jacket.

It was now a week or so before the conference. Mindy and I were again downtown. There's a Saturday sidewalk sale. I walked over to the men's store. There was my jacket on a rack with a sign, special sale $50. Naturally, I looked for John. He wasn't there. I explained the situation to the manager. He checked the records and found my deposit. His eyes bulged at the $450 balance. I decided this was an opportune time to propose a deal. I glared. "Something's not right, is it?"

He nodded.

I saw a nice burnt orange shirt and a pair of matching pants. "How about I give you another $50 in cash right now for all three items?"

I'm still thinking the outfit is cool. *After all, cool is what cool sees.*

I knew he was probably thinking, *thank you, God, for letting me get rid of this stuff.*

I didn't care. We closed the sale. Cash changed hands. He told me to wait a minute. He returned with the brightest colored tie I'd even seen.

"My gift. Goes with the outfit."

I strutted down the street with Mindy on one arm, my clothes in the other, and a big ear-to-ear grin. I thought to myself, *You've gotta get up early in the morning to outsmart old Art. A hundred bucks, and I got the coolest outfit I'd ever owned. Can't wait to see the faces on the guys and girls at the office.*

Chapter 30

Colorado Hobo

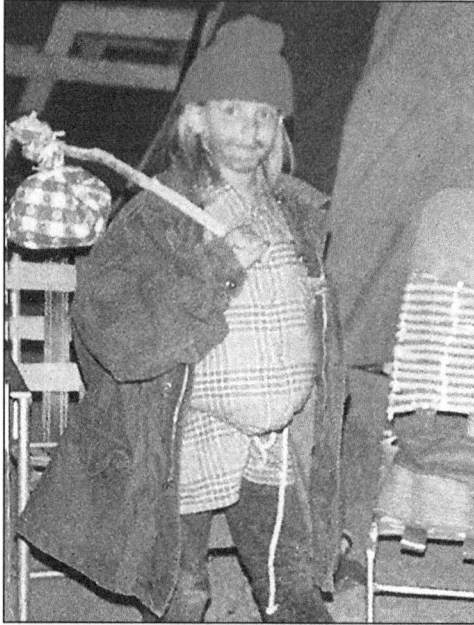

Mindy, age 8, goes trick-or-treating
at a campground near the Colorado River.

I HAD A BOAT. It was an 18-foot Ranger In/Out
Bow Rider, which meant it was a tough, little sucker.

And I had a ritual. I used to take my nephews, Royce,
Ricco, and Jack, along with Mindy up to the Black
Meadow Campground on the Colorado River, pretty
much every weekend. (Royce and Ricco were identical
twins of a most unusual sort. When full grown, Royce
turned out to be 6 foot 4 inches tall and Ricco, 5 foot 8
inches. Always wondered if some X or Y chromosomes
got mixed during the delivery).

Black Meadow was perfect for us. It was only about a
three-hour drive, had great fire pits, and a little general
store a few miles away in case you ran out of the
necessities.

They were fun times. We'd catch some fish during the day and filet them for dinner. Then we'd make stoke a nice warm campfire to take the chill out of the air and cook the fish. Sometimes, after dinner, we'd toast marshmallows, and I'd tell stories under a sky filled with twinkling stars.

This one weekend, we were a real entourage. My sister took her boys in her car. Mindy and I followed in my El Camino, pulling the boat. As always, I made a campfire. As we're sitting around, my sister said, "Know what this is?"

I thought to myself, *It's our campground. Hope she's not having a senility attack!*

"It's Halloween!"

Mindy, now eight, looked so disappointed. "I guess we won't go trick-or-treating this year." I had a guilt pang. Lori stared blankly, and my three nephews came up with an idea.

"Let's just dress Mindy in a costume. She can go trick-or-treating over there," pointing to a trailer park a few hundred yards away that was populated mostly by retirees who lived there all year round.

A decision was reached. Mindy would be a hobo. We put one of my hunting shirts on her, gave her some extra stomach padding, and covered her in my coat. It practically came down to her ankles. The boys got a stick for her to carry, put some leaves in a handkerchief, and tied it to the end of the stick.

"Something's missing," said my sister, who walked over to the campfire and picked up a piece of charred wood. She blew it cool, then drew a charcoal mustache on Mindy's face. Mindy looked hysterical standing around that fireplace. I decided to take a picture. Everybody was excited. A few minutes later, Mindy headed straight towards the lights of the trailer camp. I'm not exactly sure how long she was gone, but it seemed like forever. I started to get worried.

Suddenly, out of the dark, my munchkin appeared with a big smile.

"So how did we do? Did we get many treats?"

Mindy pulled a few pieces of candy out of her pocket. I felt terrible! All that work, all that excitement, and so little to show for it. "The people were very nice," she said. "But, they sure were surprised. One lady said I was the first hobo she had seen in years in these parts."

Suddenly it all made sense. We sent Mindy off to trick or treat in a trailer park where nobody has seen trick or treaters for years!

"I'm sorry you worked so hard. Poppy's mistake. I'll make it up to you."

She stared at me quizzically.

"Look at this," said Mindy opening her coat pocket wide. "Everybody just started giving me money." I looked in her pocket. It was full of coins.

"How much did I make, Poppy?"

I counted about eight dollars.

Mindy smiled. "And that's all mine?"

"You do the hauling," I responded, "and you get the haul."

Mindy never forgot that a little imagination and a lot of hard work can deliver unimagined good fortune

Chapter 31
Disco Dude

Beauty and the Beast.
Mindy is 13, and I'm 32, dressing and acting like 18.

WHEN IT COMES TO THE opposite sex, I've always been a contradiction in terms.

I'm social but shy. As a single man, it was not uncommon for me to dress up and sit in a popular bar by myself until some girl approached me. It didn't happen often, but that was good enough for me.

In a group, the story was a little different. I became more outgoing. I guess I felt there was safety in numbers. One Friday night, I went out with some friends from the office. There were about six of us, four men and two women. We were sitting at a table in a happening bar. I saw this knockout sitting in the lap of some guy a few tables away. I decided to buy her a drink. My friend advised me, why create trouble, there are lots of single women in the room? I told him I liked that specific gal and not to worry; I could take care of myself. I had no idea she was accompanied by this guy.

The waiter delivered the drink with my compliments. She looked over and smiled. The guy wigged out! They began to bicker. He walked off in a huff. She came over and sat in my lap. I was certain she was attracted by the cool brown suit I had just bought at Silverwood's Men's Store. It had the tightest angel flight pants you could possibly imagine. (I never wore bell bottoms. They were a little too queer for me). We had a few laughs and then went our separate ways. Her laugh reminded me of a hyena. I never saw her again.

~

Those were also the days of the disco craze. Everybody wanted to dance like John Travolta. After all, he got all the young cuties. I guess he was my role model at that point in my life. He got me interested in women that were about ten years younger. I post-rationalized that I had little in common with women my own age. To score like John, I knew I had to look the part before I could act the part with confidence. I updated my brown suit and tight pants with a white-on-white shirt that had a collar wide enough to hang-glide on and a gold chain attached to a four-pound nugget.

I can still remember the first time I stood in front of the big mirror in my bedroom. Even though I was never exactly a chick magnet, I thought I saw one, very cool disco-dude. That outfit made me feel like a dancing Superman. I imagined I could suck the chicks out of the local discos with fantastically fluid versions of the Bus Stop, the Hustle, and the Three-Step.

In reality, I had the rhythm of a tree trunk and an insecurity complex just as massive. My disco fever quickly dissipated the night a shapely, twenty-something cutie at the club told me I looked like "a one-legged monkey dancing on a cupcake."

~

A few days later, I saw an advertisement in the newspaper that Sears was having a portrait special. Just $5.95 for an 8"x10" portrait. I knew it was a promotional tease, but as a salesman myself, I knew nobody could pull the wool over my eyes. Besides, I really wanted a portrait of Mindy and me. She was growing up so fast; I wanted to capture the moment.

We head down to Sears, Mindy in her new dress and me in my disco outfit. By the time the photographer told me how cute my daughter was and what a wonderful father-daughter portrait we were going to have, I've already agreed to buy the entire package for the "promotional" price of only $150.

When the portrait arrived in the mail (see above), I jokingly named it *Beauty and the Beast*, which in hindsight wasn't too far from the truth!

~

Sometimes, I ask myself, what was the meaning of my disco period? The answer is always the same. Absolutely nothing.

Sometimes you do things that have no rhyme or reason, but you spend forever trying to figure out what nothing means.

Chapter 32

Groceries, Gas & Nash

Worn, two-toned 1956 Nash Rambler,
like the one Frank was driving back to Oregon.

THE WEEKLY BONDING-TRIP with Mindy was always a kick.

My daughter Mindy was fourteen. I'd done pretty well for a single father. She loved me, and I was crazy about her.

"Are we going grocery shopping?" she asked. I nodded. Then I sat down at the kitchen table, made a list, and estimated how much it would cost. I wanted to make sure I always carried a little extra in case we bought a few unplanned items. I've just never been a credit card kind of guy.

I took $100 out of the safe in my bedroom (in those days I was certain banks took your money but made it hard for you to get it back), and we headed off in my car. We got to a hill called Arrow Street in the City of La Verne, not far from where we were living at the time. I was about to make a left turn. Out of the corner of my eye, I spotted one of those guys with a sorrowful cardboard sign "Veteran needs gas to get home," leaning against a telephone pole. I continued to drive by, even though I knew I'm going to make a U-Turn. I wanted to see if Mindy said anything

"Poppy, did you see that guy? I think he was a veteran like you."

I was proud of her. Like her grandfather, she was generous to a fault.

We turned around and parked the car 50 yards or so from the corner. I was a little conflicted, but I didn't let on. One side of me wanted to help. The other side was convinced the guy was a scam artist. But Mindy, who doesn't have a cynical bone in her body, dove headlong into the issue. "I hope we can help," she said matter of factly as we headed toward the telephone pole. I looked into her eyes. I remember saying to myself: *I don't want my only daughter to think her father would disrespect another human being, even if he is a con artist.*

"I'm sure we can, dear," I said reassuringly.

My recollections of the next few minutes are quite vivid. The guy had a mixture of gray and black hair (mostly gray) sitting on an average build and was he dressed in black overalls dotted with rips and tears, a dark jacket, and a colored shirt. I guessed he was probably in his fifties or sixties. Man, was he tired and haggard. Big rings under his eyes. I started to ask him a few questions. It became rather clear he was genuinely hurting. He was a Vietnam veteran and had just been released from the Veterans' Hospital. "Don't walk so well from the wound," he said leaning on his cane. "Have had a bad run of luck, lost my job, don't have anybody down here. So, Ive decided to drive home and stay with some family. Would appreciate some money towards gas."

I looked around. The only car I could spot was mine. "And what do you expect to put the gas in?"

The guy looked at me quizzically. "What do you mean?"

"I mean, where's your car?"

He pointed across the street to a dirt lot. There sat the sorriest looking Nash Rambler station wagon I had ever seen. It was dusty and dirty, the body hardly had any paint remaining, and the tires were almost bald. The car was jammed with everything the guy owned. There was just enough room in the front seat for him to drive. And, absolutely no way he could ever use his rear view mirror.

After a little chatter, I learned the man's name was Frank. He was headed north to a little town in Oregon just north of Portland. "How much money do you need?"

"Twenty or thirty dollars should get me there."

I'm thinking to myself, *how could that be?*

"I get about 25 miles a gallon, and I'll sleep in the car."

"What about food?"

"I don't need to eat. I lasted longer than two days with no food in the service when my battalion got ambushed, and I hid from the Cong until reinforcements arrived."

Mindy looked at me and vice versa.

"Frank, just wait here. I've got to get something out of my car."

"Hardly going anywhere," he responded.

I got into the car and took a pen and scrap of paper from the glove compartment. I began to calculate. I figured he needed two nights at a hotel at so much. Three meals a day at so much per meal. There was no way that heap got 25 miles a gallon. I figured 20 at the most. I started adding up costs in my head, scratched them down on the paper, and totaled it up.

"How much is all that, Poppy?" asked Mindy.

"About $235," I responded.

We walked back over to Frank. I said, "Frank, based on my calculations, you really should have about $230…I pause…let's call it $250 to make sure you get home safely." He asked me how in the world I came up with that number. I explained the logic.

"I've got a hundred dollars on me that I was going to use for grocery shopping. I'd like you to have it."

He was touched by the gesture. He began to cry. Mindy cried too. I had all I could to keep my emotions under control. I didn't want to turn the event into a river of tears. I told him I had one other idea. He again agreed to await our return. Mindy and I got in the car, drove home, and took another $150 out of the safe.

Frank seemed incredulous. He couldn't thank us enough. Minutes later he got in his tattered Nash Rambler, drove across the street to the gas station, filled his car, and then drove away. We watched. He waved goodbye. I still remember his broad smile.

From time to time, I reflect on that day. I didn't think it was a big deal then, and I still don't. After all, Pop told me *generosity and compassion for other people gets returned ten-fold.*

Mindy has told the story of that day 20 years ago to all my grandchildren. "Girls, always remember, Papa Cado is a very special grandpa," she cried.

That simple sentence gave me about a 20-fold return on my money. I pray my feel grandchildren feel the same way about their very special mother.

Chapter 33

Sixteen Esmeraldas

Mindy on her 16th birthday.
She looked spectacular, and we had a hell of a time.

I WANTED MARINDA MARIE Mercado's sixteenth birthday to be something special. She had brought such joy into my life since the day she was born. To paraphrase Forrest Gump, "Me and my daughter Mindy had been like peas and carrots. They go together."

I saw this birthday as her coming of age party. She was no longer merely a teenager.

Our years together were built on a foundation of trust, reasonableness and a sense of responsibility. I never raised my hand, it wasn't necessary. In fact, I remember chewing her out unfairly one time. After I dropped her off at school, I felt just terrible. I sat brooding at my desk for almost 30 minutes. I decided to do the proper thing. I drove back to school, walked into the principal's office, explained the situation, and asked if we could get Mindy out of class, so that I could apologize to her.

Minutes later, we were standing in the school hallway. "I'm, sorry, honey. My outburst was terribly wrong and out of all proportion. I promise I'll never do that again."

She looked into my eyes, then hugged and kissed me. Nothing more needed to be said. I've kept that promise to this day.

~

Mindy always knew I was there for her. No matter how small or big the issue.

From the time she was about five, she gave me cards for Mother's Day, Father's Day, Valentine's Day, Easter and whatever. She would write different personalized messages in each card, but they were all signed the same, "Poppy, thanks for being there through the little things and the big ones."

I mean, what more could a father ask for? I still have every one of those cards. Every now and then, I reread them. It makes me feel like I did okay. I'm certain Mindy realizes intuitively how important those cards are to me because she never forgets to add to my collection, even though she's a busy lady with four kids of her own.

~

Mindy had grown into a real lady right before my eyes. So, I decided her 16th birthday should be a "grown-up date."

The evening's festivities started with a three-course dinner for the two of us in the Emerald Room at the Candle Lite Pavilion (which normally held eight people), followed by a performance of *The King and I* from our private box in the balcony.

(Mindy had already developed a fondness for emeralds and theatrical musicals).

"Poppy, you're the best," she said, when I told her about the plans. Her response made me feel like a million bucks.

During the day, I took her shopping for a grown-up dress. After trying on a few outfits, she appeared in front of me in a sculpted black evening dress. Two thoughts raced through my mind: My baby was gone. A beautiful woman with blond hair cascading down the soft chiffon stood in her place.

My second thought? If any guy so much as touched my daughter, I'd bust his gut!

I realized my birthday gift had to be as special as the evening. I decided to give my daughter her first piece of real jewelry, an emerald and diamond ring.

When Mindy opened the box, her blue eyes twinkled like stars in the heavens.

From that day forward, whenever the mood struck me, I would buy Mindy an expensive piece of jewelry. I figured I didn't have a wife, and money was for spending. Before long, she had quite a collection of bling. She thought nothing of wearing the stuff everywhere, which started to concern me. Suppose her friends thought she was trying to show them up? One day I gingerly broached the subject. "Mindy, aren't you concerned your friends will think you're a little spoiled?"

She looked at me like I was a man from Mars.

"Spoiled about what?"

"I mean wearing expensive jewelry all the time."

She laughed. "Not a chance, Poppy, all my friends think it's costume jewelry."

Mindy's innocent response reinforced something my Pop taught me a long time ago. *Money was never meant for showing off.*

Chapter 34

Five By-Pass

My first major surgery.
A five passage open heart procedure that took 8 hours.

THE FIRST 40 YEARS OF my life I thought I was invincible. But that changed rather quickly on August 2, 1990.

Mindy was away visiting her mother, and I was getting ready for work. I had just put on my dress shirt and was tying my tie. Suddenly, I had a pain in my jaw that was so severe I thought I was going to implode.

On reflection, I had been experiencing pains in my chest on and off for a few weeks. I just never told Mindy because I figured they'd somehow go away. I also didn't want her to take my cigarettes, which I hide under my bed.

I fell to the floor. I knew I had a heart attack. I pulled myself up and got to the phone. I called the Pomona

Valley Hospital. The voice on the other end said, "Sorry for the delay, we are quite busy at the moment." Then, she put me on hold!

The pain struck again, with even more intensity. It was like nothing I'd ever experienced. This time I pulled the cord, and the phone fell to the floor near me. I dialed the hospital again. Again, they put me on hold!

I figured I had two options: Lie on the floor and die, or get my butt into my demo car, and drive several miles to the car dealership where I worked, so that somebody could get me to the emergency room. I chose the latter option. I don't remember how I got up and out the door. But I do remember stopping at the mirror in the front hall and fixing my tie. Not long after, I staggered into my sales manager's office. "Bill, I'm having a heart attack. Take me to the hospital."

He jumped out of his seat and rushed me to Foothill Hospital a few miles away. He pulled right up to the front door. I told him to pull around back near the emergency room, "I don't want to make a fuss; for Christ's sake, it's only a heart attack!"

He told me I was crazy, but he humored me. I guess he figured arguing with a stubborn mule like me would only make things worse. I told him, "Bill, I'm fine; go park the car. I'll get myself inside. By the time you get to the front desk, I'll have a good idea when you should come back to pick me up." I staggered to a desk where two nurses were sitting. I whispered quietly, "I think I've had a heart attack." All hell broke loose. Doctors were being paged; I was on a gurney with an oxygen mask, IV's were being inserted into my veins, a nitro pill was placed under my tongue, and there was this nurse bending over me trying to take off my tie.

"Blood pressure 220/152, pulse highly irregular," I heard faintly. They spent the next five hours trying to stabilize me. I was still in severe pain. I'm moved to ICU. The doctor huddled in the corner. "Mr. Mercado, our only option is to give you an experimental drug treatment."

"Bring it on," I responded. The next thing I knew I was sucking some liquid out of a capsule. I remember it had an unpleasant burnt orange taste. My blood pressure dropped almost immediately, and the pain subsided.

The doctor told me my "veins were weak." I needed an angiogram to find out what precisely was the damage level and what next steps should be taken. "Unfortunately, Mr. Mercado, we do not have that equipment here. So, in the morning, we will be moving you to Covina Intercommunity Hospital, which specializes in cardiovascular disease. But Nurse Frahunter will monitor you closely throughout the night."

I nodded. This drop-dead gorgeous, red-haired angel of mercy smiled at me. My veins perked up, and, despite the day's chaos, I slept soundly, knowing Nurse Frahunter was by my side.

Oh, I forgot to mention a little bit of my prior background. About two years before, I had a routine physical. You know lab results, etc., etc. The doctor called me at work the next day. "Mr. Mercado, your cholesterol is an astronomical 350 +. All your other statistics (triglycerides, HDL, LDL's) are also horrible. If we don't do something about it, and quick, you are going to die."

The doctor wanted to change my diet and put me on a collection of medications. Reluctantly, I agreed to eat salads for a while with no-fat dressing, but I refused the medications. I told him, "I've heard about those crazy side effects." Never really went to that doctor, or any doctor, again. I just assumed life would go on the way it does.

The next day, I was moved to Covina Intercommunity. Something told me I better get my affairs in order. I explained to the staff, "Before we do the angiogram, I need to take care of some matters at the house." Unbeknownst to me, Bill contacted my daughter and told her to get down to the hospital right away and talk some sense into her crazy old man.

The next morning, we did an angiogram with Mindy by my side. I noticed this guy standing behind her. I figured he was a tech or something. I'm lying on a cold stainless-steel table. We all looked up at a monitor indicating five blocked arteries. "Mr. Mercado, this is quite serious. I don't remember the last time I saw the need for a five-bypass. We should operate immediately."

Mindy clutched my hand. The way I saw it, these guys were chomping at the bit to dive into my chest. "Wait a minute, Doc, not so fast," I protested. I want to get a second opinion."

"You want a second opinion?" said the doctor. "You're going to die. That's the second opinion. In fact, even if we start right now you've only got about a ten percent chance."

"Poppy, please," begged Mindy. "You've got to do this for me."

I looked into her eyes. I figured a 10 percent shot was at least 10 percent better than dead.

I nodded affirmatively. The guy standing behind Mindy turned out to be the anesthesiologist. I'm zonked out a split second later. Eight hours later, I wake thirsty as hell. Unfortunately, I've got a steel pipe down my throat. And the chunky nurse hovering over me, monitoring my every movement, looked nothing like Nurse Frahunter, if you get my drift.

(If you look closely at the medical sheet at the front of this chapter, you'll notice I was on life support for more than two hours and never needed so much as a pint of blood. The doctors were amazed).

Ten days later I left the hospital. I was feeling damn good. The doctors prescribed a 16-week recovery period. I visited my cardiologist's office one week later. I told him, "I'm ready to go back to work." He told me I was crazy. "You're an invalid."

I walked him into his waiting room. "Let me show you something, Doc. These are the invalids you need to worry about." He shook his head but gave me my release.

Two weeks later I was back selling cars alongside Bill. My little five-bypass taught me some important things: *Non-fat dressings don't work."*

"Don't ask for second opinions when you're dying."

"Never lose faith, no matter how the odds are stacked."

~

About six weeks later, I'm playing left field in a pick-up baseball game at the park near my house. Nobody knows there are playing with an invalid!

During the first few innings, I swung the bat confidently, but a little more slowly than usual. In the fourth inning, the batter hit a short fly ball in my direction. The shortstop backed up and shouted, "I've got it. I've got it." I figured he did, so I get the hell out of the way, rather than risk a collision. I was so confident he's on the chase, I didn't even look up for the ball. A split second later he lost the ball in the sun, and it crashed smack-dab in the middle of my chest. I felt something pop. I thought *cracked bone*. But something felt like it was pushing against the inside of my skin, and it hurt like hell.

I went right back to my cardiologist. He examined me, took some x-rays and laughed at the findings. I said, "Doc, what's so funny?"

"It appears one or two of the wires we inserted to hold your chest cavity together after the five-bypass, have snapped."

I panicked. "God, now what?" Thinking the Doc was going to open me up again.

"Nothing," said the Doctor. "The bone will grow back over the breaks. In the meantime, I'll just push the wire back in place, so it's not rubbing against your skin." He did so. I yelped. The pain subsided almost immediately.

I haven't played baseball since, and the wires have never pressed against my skin again. I think.

Part Three

Love Arrives

Chapter 35

Part-Time Cowboy

From $500 sports coats and disco dude to
Hopalong Cassidy and Gene Autry.

MY DNA HAS ALWAYS contained cowboy genes.

To begin with, I was just a poor kid born and raised in Mobile, Alabama, with Roy Rodgers on the television and Eddy Arnold and Patsy Cline singing in the background. And, Mom played a steel guitar and sang in a country band before she met Pop.

So, it was only natural that when I reached my forties and was divorced and selling cars, I would become a part-time cowboy!.

One Friday night, my friend Bill said, "Artie, what say we go to a Western bar I know in San Dimas. It's only about fifteen minutes from here. Great music and very friendly women." (Bill always drove fast cars, made big money, thought he knew the happening places, liked shortcuts, and young, friendly ladies).

We walked into a second-floor establishment called the Western Connection in traditional *Yankee business attire* —suits, shirts, and ties. Everybody in the joint smirked and stared; I felt completely and utterly out of place. I also noticed something else—the women outnumbered the men about 4 to 1, and they were fine!

Saturday morning, Bill and I paid a visit to the Western clothing store on the first floor, directly below the bar. They had quite a variety of the coolest cowboy gear like Gene Autry elaborately trimmed shirts like Gene Autry, big brass Tom Mix belt buckles, and boots with intricate designs that would have made Roy Rogers and Dale Evans proud.

I decided to go the whole nine yards: side stitch Levi's, blue shirt, designer boots, brass buckle belt, and a big black felt Resistol 4X cowboy hat that cost $157, which was a hell of a lot of money for a working stiff back then. We finished shopping about 11 a.m., and headed back to work selling cars, motivated to pay for all the stuff we had bought. About 9 p.m., we closed the showroom, got dressed like cowboys, and headed back to the bar, acting like regulars.

We notice some things we had missed on our aborted visit the previous night. The place was enormous with a big bar overlooking a huge dance floor. I quickly discovered the girls expected you to dance with them if you wanted to meet them. The problem was, even if I wanted to try, the band didn't play any dances I knew. Their repertoire focused on stuff like the Cotton Eye Joe, the cowboy cha-cha, the ten-step, the cowboy waltz, and the worst of the batch, the west coast swing. I realized I was a fish out of water. Big time!

I retired to one end of the bar with a beer while Bill decided to try his hand at dancing. He wasn't very good, but he didn't seem to care. Neither did the girls.

The music stopped. He walked over to me. "I'd really like to get to know this girl I've been dancing with, but she's with a girlfriend, so you gotta help me out." I shook my head no. Big bad Arthur was frightened to death of embarrassing himself on the dance floor.

The band guy announced, "Tonight there are free dance lessons." He urged all the cowpokes to get a partner, come out on the floor, and learn a few dances compliments of Brian and Candy, whoever the hell they were! Bill introduced me to Sally, and Sally introduced me to Linda, who introduced me to the dance floor. She gently took my hand and pulled me toward the floor.

She started laughing before we ever got there. "Your hand is shaking."

"Yours would be too if you were me."

She smiled again. I acquiesced to her charms. That first night I didn't do well on the dance floor, but I found Linda cute and fun. It turned out she was an executive at General Dynamics, had two boys, and was into antiques.

"What's a girl like you doing in a place like this?" I asked a little later.

"I like to play cowgirl," she smiled.

I decided that was the last time I was going to be embarrassed with Linda on the dance floor. The next day I convinced dance instructors, Brian and Candy, to give Bill and me private lessons before the place opened. We kept taking lessons until we were at least respectable. That took several weeks.

I didn't exactly become Arthur Murray, but at least I could do a few basic dances without stepping all over Linda's feet. Before long, Linda and I and Bill and Sally became regulars at the Western Connection. The four of us even had our own ringside table when the big acts like Pam Tillis came to town.

With Linda's encouragement, I became considerably less self-conscious on the dance floor. I would pretty much try anything the band threw at us, except for line-dancing. I thought that was strictly for sissies. One night, Linda, Sally, and Bill all decided to line-dance. I took a pass and decided to walk over to the bar and get another beer. I stood next to this mountain of a man. I decided to break the ice.

"Can you believe those guys line-dancing? That's strictly for women and queers."

The guy stared down at me. "Don't know about that. I like to line-dance."

I decided to walk away.

~

When we weren't socializing at the Connection, Linda was organizing all kinds of Western activities: a country dance in Palm Springs, a Bluegrass Festival in the mountains, Hal Ketchum concerts, a trip to the Gene Autry Museum in Griffith Park, etc. She was the engine in our relationship. I was just the caboose that went along for the ride.

Linda was more than just a ball of energy; she was generous to a fault. Seemed like every time she went on a business trip, she'd bring me back a cowboy shirt or something. One Christmas she bought me the black suede jacket you see in the picture at the front of this chapter. She always wanted to dress her cowboy. On a typical evening, I'd show up in elk skin cowboy boots (they were good for dancing), the finest Resistol 4X felt cowboy hat, fancy shirt, tapered pants, and a silver belt buckle. Between what I bought and what Linda bought me, my closets were loaded. I was officially a part-time cowboy with a not-so-pretty face. Before we'd go out, I'd look at myself in the mirror and say, "Arthur, you're a fine-looking cowboy." Linda would just laugh.

Unfortunately, our relationship ended abruptly. She said General Dynamics was closing in San Diego, and that she had been asked by the company to take a big position in Arizona. She wanted me to come with her. She explained after 20 plus years, she couldn't say no because *our* retirement account would take a big hit. It was a great compliment; after all, she was a classy lady, who had taken me out of my shell forever.

I thought long and hard. I knew she loved me without reservation. I tried to love her, but I just couldn't and didn't. At least, not in the way she wanted. So, I declined.

After she left, we talked a few times on the phone. But gradually, the calls became fewer and far between. I didn't go to the Western Connection anymore, and I didn't go to Country and Western festivals. The Cowboy left. It didn't fit anymore. I kept a few of my cowboy duds. Kind of a reminder of a passage in my life.

Chapter 36

Bicycles 'n Nuggets

My little issue was wrapped in fun packaging.

MY PROPENSITY TO GAMBLE started innocently enough.

During high school, my all-time favorite card game was called Between-the-Sheets. Everybody put some money in the pot and was dealt two cards face up. Then you declared how much of the pot you were going for and drew a third card.

If that card had a value between the other cards, you took the declared amount from the pot. If the third card wasn't Between-the-Sheets, you had to add your declared amount to the pot. Sometimes that pot contained $40 or $50, which was big money for a bunch of 17-year-olds back then. We all won some and lost some but always came back for more.

~

I quit college early, completed my unbelievable five-month stint in the Army, and started to date Lynn, a fun-loving girl who lived next store. We went camping, fishing, hiking, and boating, and laughed a lot. A few years later, we got married, had or daughter, Mindy.

A couple of times a year, Lynn and I made like tourists and drove to downtown Las Vegas, grabbed a meal and did some penny-ante gambling—$30 or less! Like the high school poker games at my house, I'd win some and lose some, but the urge to go further was very much under control.

One afternoon, we arrived in Vegas with the usual $30 in my pocket. I figured we'd stay for three or four hours then return home. I told Lynn I was tired, so maybe we should stay the night. "But we don't have the money," she said. I told her just to hang out in the lobby while I headed to the blackjack table to win a few hands. Fifteen minutes later, we had stay-over money. She smiled approvingly.

We both started to get hungry. I again returned to the table, won a little more. We had a nice dinner. As we walked around the casino shops, Lynn saw this charming, colorful hand-painted doll. Yup, you've got it. Back to the tables. By now, I'd concluded this gambling thing was a cinch. If I paid attention, I couldn't lose. In the morning, we headed back to California with Lynn's new doll, full stomachs, and a couple of hundred dollars in my pocket.

Things eventually don't work out with Lynn and I became a single guy with a daughter. Like I said in an earlier chapter, I got a job selling insurance at the Auto Club. That's where I first met Rick. Nice guy, fellow salesman. Rick invited me to the Commerce Poker Club on the outskirts of L.A. Unbeknownst to me at the time; Rick was an avid gambler. Next thing I know, I'm enjoying the action that first night. I win a bunch of money. Rick lost his shirt. He was one depressed dude. Privately, on the way home, I convinced myself that poker was even easier to play and win than blackjack. In retrospect, that should have been my personal warning light.

Time flew. Mindy was now in her senior year of high school, and I was consistently near or at the head of the Auto Club's leader board. I also became a regular at the Bicycle Casino, a gambling parlor about 40 minutes from where we lived at the time. I figured I could spend a few hours gambling and still be around for Mindy. The casino had great food and a very social atmosphere. It was there I realized my mind was like a human calculator. I could identify possible outcomes and likely odds in a nanosecond before I placed a bet or raised the ante. While my means did not allow me to become a real high-roller, I was now well hooked on gambling. I also was a master at justifying my urge to gamble: I needed a sociable release from the pressures of work; I wanted nothing but the best for Mindy, I wanted to spoil my second wife, Rosie, who clearly loved the finer things in life.

~

I began to visit Vegas with increasing frequency. Eventually, I decided the Golden Nugget Saloon and Casino was the classiest place in town (remember, this was before the Strip expanded). My appetite to score grew. I started playing for bigger pots: $2,000 to $5,000 buy-ins were now the norm. I wasn't what you'd call a regular, but the staff knew me by name, and the freebies flowed–rooms, meals, drinks, the whole nine yards. I felt comfortable and important, just like at the Bicycle Casino. When I crossed the border into Nevada, I felt the adrenalin rush.

I also came to recognize the pattern of the typical out-of-control gambler. When they won a big pot, they would hold a tiny portion aside and confidently risk the rest. In reality, they always lost more than they won and usually wound up in a bigger hole. Then, they'd start borrowing money to win the big pot that would put them in the black and make everything right. Ultimately, losing would put a significant dent in their dignity, and they would lie to anyone and everybody to save face–the truth was just too painful.

I convinced myself that I wasn't out-of-control despite the fact that when I won big, I took most of my winnings off the table, and eventually lost a lot more than I won. *Gambling is a lot like playing golf. You may have a dreadful round, but you remember the good holes, which keeps you coming back for another round.*

Gamblers remember the big pots. I won $4,800 in roulette. In fact, I can still remember my big score as clearly as yesterday. I had $317 in my pocket when I arrived. I played poker at the $10-$20 table. I was hot. It was $1,500 then $2,000. The pit boss Matt walked by. I told him you've got to do me a favor. "I'm smoking. You've got to get me into the Dragon Room." (The high-roller spot where bets started at $400). He obliged. In a matter of hours, I walk out with $22,000 in the top of my socks and all four pant pockets.

I went home, paid all my outstanding bills, which had started to mount—despite my rather substantial income —bought Mindy a car and Rosie some baubles.

~

Finally, my worst nightmare arrived. The night that broke the camel's back. I was playing a game called Pan 9. The object was to place your bets and try to get as close to nine as possible. I drew a card. It made me an eight under the rules of the game.

I was certain I was going to take the first four guys at the table. (Based on the odds, that hand usually wins 90% of the time). The person to my left makes a nine. I'm surprised. The next two players also make nines. I'm flabbergasted. Even the pit boss couldn't believe what he had just witnessed. When the dust settled, I lost the entire $10,000 that I had banked. The odds of that are probably somewhere north of ten-million-to-one.

As I stood silently at the table, I was disgusted with the intensity of my greed. I was out of control. I had bottomed out. I was angry with myself, embarrassed. Suddenly, one of Pop's lessons of life popped into my head, *never lose your self-dignity. It's what makes a man a man.*

I knew what I had to do. I looked at the dealer, Matt. I handed him a $100 tip and said, "You won't be seeing me for a while."

For the next several months, I worked hard to regain control of my life. Some gamblers have support systems. I didn't. When I asked Rosie for financial support, she told me "no." That gambling was my problem, not hers. Then she left.

While the rejection was unpleasant, I had no one to blame but myself. I had taken three steps back, financially and otherwise. I became my own support group. I decided never again to allow the urge to gamble dominate me. It's 25 years later, and life is good.

Chapter 37

My Last Date

When it comes to women,
I learned you can't tell a book by its cover. Ever.

LINDA WAS HISTORY, I WAS in my late forties and felt dreadfully alone. I was also starting to have chronic health problems. Nothing major, a little pain in my chest here, and a twinge in my jaw there. I typically ignored the signals, and the pain passed. Of course, in retrospect, it was six or seven years since the five by-pass, and certain arteries were starting to re-clog.

Mindy, now 19, and I rented a lovely two-story house on the top of Chino Hills. She was dating guys but not finding the right one, and I wasn't doing so well on the women front either. I decided to let my friends talk me into a few blind dates.

~

My friend Frank's wife, Gloria, was a knock-out. Perfect figure, pretty as a picture, and a bubbly personality to match. She called and said, "Arthur, I have this friend, Barbara. She's perfect. She's good-looking, intelligent, and fun." (You know all the usual stuff girls say about other girls). "I've already talked to her about you. She's waiting for your call."

My first thought was I don't do *blind dates, that's like playing craps with one die.* My second thought was, I can't disappoint Gloria. Barbara sounded nice enough on the phone, but just in case, I told her I was limited on time because this was the peak selling season at the showroom. We agreed to a one-hour Sunday brunch.

I arrived first. In walked this woman who didn't look a day *over 65.* She came over to the table, smiled, and introduced herself as Barbara. She was pleasant enough but I thought to myself, *do I call her Barbara, mom or grandma?* I was out of there in precisely 59 minutes, with a vague, "I'll call you."

The only call I made was to Gloria. I asked her in what decade was Barbara "good-looking." That was terribly rude.

~

My second blind date was initially a lot more promising.

Another referral from the wife of a friend. This time I saw a picture first. Joanne was a knock-out. I decided to meet her at the romantic landmark hotel in Riverside, the Mission Inn. But, as always, for insurance purposes, I explained I could only spend about an hour over cocktails because I was working the evening shift on the showroom floor. She understood.

When she walked in, she lit up the room. The picture didn't do her justice. She was petite, good-looking, and soft-spoken. Style, class, and grace—she was the whole package.

She told me I am even more handsome than my picture. I smile, "I guess your beautiful eyes aren't so good." She laughed.

Within minutes, we're talking, drinking, and really clicking. She looked at her watch. "The hour's almost up, don't you have to go back to work?" I told her to wait a minute. I headed for the phone and called Mindy at home to tell her I'm having a good time. I returned to the table with a big smile on my face, "We're in luck, one of my friends said he'd cover my shift."

We had dinner and were giggling and holding hands like teenagers by the time we got back to her place. I really liked her. Nothing happened that first evening; we just sat and talked and got to know each other.

We had a few more dates. Everything was going great; we graduated to a more intimate stage.

It was close to Christmas. We were having dinner in a quiet, romantic, candlelit restaurant. She asked, "What are *we* doing for Christmas?"

I'm a little taken back. I explained nicely that I'm a single parent and always spend the holiday with my daughter and my sister. I told Joanne I thoroughly enjoyed her company and wanted to get to know her better, but that I was a little beyond that love-at-first-sight stuff.

There was dead silence. She stared for what seemed like an eternity; then she went completely ballistic. It was like I was suddenly sitting across the table from Dr. Jekyll and Mr. Hyde's sister. I remained calm. The calmer I remained, the more upset she became. I realized I was sitting across the table from a Tasmanian Devil! She remained psycho for another few minutes. Everybody in the place was staring. As far as I was concerned, the lights were out. I'm thinking God only knows how long it would have been before she tried to kill my daughter and told me she went on a trip.

I paid the bill, we got into the car, and she became apologetic. She kept talking. I didn't say a word. I couldn't wait to dump her at her house. (When I used to get angry at a woman, and that wasn't often, I'd just clam up. As far as I was concerned, she had just hit her real inner personality, and I was out of there).

Anyway, back to my friend. Joanne called me a few more times to apologize. I said very little. She stopped calling. I think she finally figured, she was done, no matter what she said or did.

~

That was my last blind date. Ever. *No matter how lonely you feel, be wary of well-meaning friends offering companionship with the "perfect" blind date. It's usually they who are blind.*

Chapter 38

Laura Mitchell

Laura Mitchell introduced me to Susan, and Mindy to Jimmy.

I'M NOW 50 AND CERTAIN I don't want to be alone. At the same time, I've had no luck with the traditional dating scene. I seemed attracted to the ones who weren't really interested in me, while the ones that were seemed to have issues. One date told me I was a difficult communicator. "Getting three sentences in a row out of you is a full-time job." Another suggested I struck her as a little angry inside. "You're somebody a girl has got to think twice about taking home to meet the parents."

To make matters worse, despite being beautiful and smart, Mindy was not doing much better in the relationship department. My impression was that my bright, smart, beautiful daughter was dating mostly chumps. I just couldn't tell her that.

It was 7 p.m., I'd just finished eating one of those frozen meals and was about to turn on the TV and become a couch potato for the rest of the evening. For some reason, I decided to thumb through the sports section of the newspaper. There was this matchmaker ad by a company called Laura Mitchell Introductions. (This is before the Internet match-making craze). You can imagine the headline: "Too busy to find the right woman? Tired of the traditional dating game?"

I thought to myself, *what the hell have I got to lose*. I decided to call the phone number the next day and make an appointment. The office was pleasant enough. A woman escorted me into her office. I'm a salesman myself, so I knew it was pitch and close time.

She explained the process. "You provide us with all the relevant personal information for somebody to get a feel for who you are, what interests you. We also do a videotape.

"Assuming you qualify (good reverse close), you become a Laura Mitchell Club member. Your information will be exposed to women with similar interests, and you get to review our female members. It's all very discreet. You make the decision on whether you wish to meet the person you selected. We set the stage by letting them know you will be calling. Then the rest is up to you."

The process sounded harmless enough. "And, how much does this discretion cost?" I joked.

"There's a one-time charge of $1,800 for a two-year membership. There are no other hidden fees."

I assumed she's just throwing out the "retail" number. As a salesman, you never paid retail. I let my jaw drop for effect, then I just stared. "You've got to be kidding!"

I had seen women shudder at my stare. I realized she was intimidated. She took one more weak swing at full price. "Mr. Mercado, there's a lot of prep work and managing our portfolio…"

I respectfully interrupted. "Madame, I appreciate what you're saying, but $1,800 is out of my range."

We spent the next 15 minutes negotiating. In the end, I agreed to a $1,000 fee and got the payments spread over 12 months with no interest. I took the paperwork home to fill out my membership questionnaire. The phone rang. It was Laura Mitchell's office manager.

"Mr. Mercado, you've been selected as one of our pre-pay candidates."

I smelled desperation. "We were reviewing the records of those using our extended-pay plan and are willing to offer a 10 percent discount for those wishing to pay their membership in one lump sum." A few minutes later, we agreed on a 20 percent discount. I dropped the cash off the next morning.

~

The books weren't bad. Most the women were attractive and appeared to lead interesting lives.

Before I knew it, a few candidates had expressed interest in meeting me. I'm a little gun-shy based on my past history. I meet one for coffee and another for a drink. I figure if I like the coffee one, I can invite her to lunch, and if I like the drink one, I can invite to dinner. They were both nice, but there were no sparks; consequently, there were no lunches or dinners. They both seemed to understand.

Not long after, I brought Mindy with me to look at my latest candidate options. Mindy was impressed by the professional and discreet nature of the process. I spotted this one lady. I loved her eyes and her smile. I reviewed her information. Her name was Susan. She was well-educated and of the appropriate age range. I turned to Mindy, "So what do you think?"

Mindy tapped the page and smiled, "Pop, I think we should look at the videotape."

A few minutes into the tape and I'm intrigued. Unless my instincts had dulled, she appeared to be a real lady. I'm informed that she had also expressed an interest in meeting me. I gave her a call. I'm not my usual self. I was chatty, articulate and enjoyable. We talked for almost 45 minutes, which was a record for me. I decided to take the ultimate gamble. I invited her out to dinner, no coffee or drinks preliminary. (Turned out she hadn't had much luck on the singles scene either. She told the Laura Mitchell people she just wanted to meet a nice companion).

It turned out to be the best first date I'd had in quite some time. It was near Halloween, so we walked through a few shops on the Long Beach Pier looking at ghosts and goblins. She told me one of them looked a lot like me. We laughed. I bought her a seashell in a frame with the poem, "The Legend of the Sand Dollar."

There's a little legend
that I would like to tell
of the birth and death of Jesus
found in this lowly shell.
If you examine closely
you'll see that you find here
four nail holes and a fifth one
made by a Roman's spear.
On one side the Easter Lily
its center is the star
that appeared unto the shepherds
and led them from afar.
The Christmas poinsettia
etched on the other side
reminds us of his birthday
our happy Christmastide.
Now break the center open
and here you will release
the five white doves awaiting
to spread good will and peace.
This simple little symbol
Christ left for you and me
to help us spread his gospel
through all eternity.

We continued our walk past every shop, every game, every ride until we reached the landmark restaurant, Whiskey Pete's, at pier's end. We watched the sunset over drinks and dinner, and I read the poem. Something told me, then and there, I was going to get to know Susan better. A whole lot better. I think she felt the same.

As it turned out, I never dated another Laura Mitchell introduction. But I did apply the main lesson learned from my gambling years: *when you're on a hot streak, take your winnings off the table and play with the house's money.*

~

Mindy was fond of Susan from the get-go. She watched our relationship unfold as she continued to date, what I would call "chumps." I know Mindy was impressed with Poppy's results because, unbeknownst to me, she decided to sign up with Laura Mitchell. Shortly after that, she was introduced to Jimmy. Not long after, they got married. Mindy called Jimmy "her dream come true." I just think he's a caring husband, a great son-in-law, and a wonderful father.

Knowing how I raised Mindy, I was confident she got discount off the Laura Mitchell retail membership fee, just like her Poppy. But, I never asked her how much, and I never disclosed my deal. I saw no reason to put down my precious "pooh" (the nickname I gave Mindy a long, long time ago) because she wasn't an experienced negotiator.

(Editor's Note: Ironically, Arthur's reluctance to reveal his rock-bottom negotiated price was a blessing in disguise. Unbeknownst to her Poppy, Mindy had negotiated the Laura Mitchell fee down to $400. She never told Poopy, until recently, because she didn't want to burst "the great negotiator's" bubble).

Chapter 39

Just Say It

Susan, the love of my life, my best friend, my partner.

I WAS IN DANGEROUS WATERS with Susan, and I wasn't sure what to do.

We began dating exclusively for the next year and a half until the "Just Say It" event.

Sometimes we'd do something simple like sit around and watch TV. Those were the good old days when Artie would just call Domino's and have them deliver a pepperoni pizza with extra cheese. When it wasn't pizza, we'd get some big ice-cream sundaes at the local Baskin-Robbins.

We not only loved the same foods, but we also loved the same music—particularly Michael Crawford and *Phantom of the Opera, Lion King,* and gospel music ("Amazing Grace" was/is her favorite song). I also noticed we enjoyed doing the same things, like going to the opera, seeing concerts, and cruising around the Mexican Riviera. But, most of all, I came to enjoy her dry, witty sense of humor, and ladylike demeanor.

Heck, she even found my weird sense of humor, illogical phraseology, and quirky musical catalog "interesting." (If I really like a song, I'd record it multiple times on the same CD. The more copies I make, the more I like the song. I call it "Artie's Hit Parade." Despite my precise copy process, I never actually labeled the CD's, playing my CD's were like open a Mexican pinata.

One day she noticed I had copied Sarah Brightman and Andrea Bocelli singing "Time to Say Goodbye" five times and Bob Seger's "Against the Wind" three. "Five times," she laughed, "We must especially like that one."

~

During the courting period, we became take-out dinner junkies. Boston Market was a favorite. Pleasant ambiance, fast service, and fair prices. And, boy oh boy, I loved those sodium-laden meatloaf sandwiches and the greasy half roast chicken with stuffing and the fixings. There was only one culinary ground rule: no In-N-Out Burger double-doubles. Susan felt the quality didn't live up to their hype. I disagreed. There was, and still is, nothing quite like a double-double cheeseburger smothered in fried onions accompanied by a large order of fries and a thick shake. However, I learned painfully from my previous relationships that *there is a time to say your piece and a time to keep your mouth shut.*

~

Susan's gentle, loving manner also transformed me into Mr. Sensitivity. I became a flower-buying machine for special occasions—like the anniversary of when we met —and for lots of other "just becauses." Sometimes I sent them, sometimes I delivered them personally. I was doing my best to be a contemporary kind of guy—no red roses, that's for Moms. There were yellow roses, white lilies, purple irises, and multi-colored bouquets. She loved them all...I think. One day, after the delivery of some spectacular Casablanca lilies, she said, "Arthur, I love the flowers and the thoughtfulness, but is there some reason why you never send me red roses?"

So, I changed gears, for the next few months everything was red roses. She seemed deliriously happy.

One day over dinner, she asked sweetly, "Arthur, I love the red roses, but the occasional surprise would be nice." (Like the book says, "Men are from Mars and Women are from Venus!)

~

One night, I was home alone reading the newspaper. (At this point, Susan and I still lived separately, but I'm a regular at her place doing kissy-face and other stuff).

I thought she went shopping with her girlfriends—I never understood that shopping thing where you just look at stuff. Guys buy, girls look!

I saw an ad for a barbershop quartet for hire. I thought to myself, how cool is that? I decided Valentine's Day was fast approaching and I wanted to do something different. I called the number and hired the guys to serenade Susan at the office. I called one of her co-workers to help me get the guys into the building. It was one of those high-security office towers.

I hid by a small window looking into the open floor where Susan worked. They let the quartet in and called her name over the intercom. She came to the front, wondering what was up. One member of the barbershop quartet handed her a single red rose with my Valentine's Day greeting and began to sing "Moon River" and "You are My Sunshine." By the time the quartet finished the second song, everyone in the place was standing around Susan and cheering. She was embarrassed. I loved it. When they finished, I entered the lobby area. She gave me a big hug and a kiss. I heard a few of the girls say, "How romantic. I wish my boyfriend would do something like that for me."

I figured I did good. Susan announced in front of everybody, "Arthur, you did very well. I love you." While I felt the same, I just smiled and nodded. Still had to be careful about getting trapped in that love thing.

~

By now I knew Susan was the woman of my forever dreams. I also knew I had real health issues, so I decided I should give her the chance to opt out. I owed that to her.

"Susan," I said over dinner the next evening, "Maybe it's not so smart to get involved with a guy with a bad ticker?"

She smiled and looked right into my eyes. "I'm already involved."

I tried another tact.

"Another thing, I don't have a big savings account or retirement nest egg. When I had that five-bypass some eight years back, the doctor told me I only had a 10 percent chance of living, so I either spent the money or gave some rather generous gifts to my daughter, grandkids, and sister."

She beamed. "So your kindness has a cost."

I kept making excuses.

"You know my angina attacks are getting more frequent; I probably need to change my entire diet. No more take-outs."

She leaned over and kissed me gently. "So, no more bonbons." (I loved chocolate ice cream bonbons. Still do, although I haven't tasted one in years).

I tossed one more curve ball, "You know, you're not getting the best part of this bargain."

"Yes, I am."

Then she sat waiting patiently for my next sentence. I loved her madly, but my tongue was locked in place. Expressing affection verbally is not one of my strong points. I said something brilliant like, "I think I better get going; I've got the early shift at the showroom tomorrow."

We knew I was trying hard to avoid the obvious. We got to the door of her place door. I kissed her goodnight. She looked into my eyes and said sweetly, "Do you love me?"

I said nothing.

"Arthur," she repeated, "Do you love me?"

Again, I was verbally paralyzed.

She asked one more time. Now frustrated by my silence, she got right in my face. "Arthur, you know you love me; just say it!"

At that point, I had no alternative.

"Alright, alright. I do…I do."

"Do what?' she persisted.

"I do love you."

The rest is history.

~

It's become a lot easier to tell Susan I love her now. In fact, I do it all the time. *I guess if you love somebody without reservation, it's not going to hurt anymore if you admit it sooner rather than later. If they love you, you've saved time. If they don't, you can get on with your life.*

Chapter 40

Lion and Lamb

One of my first gifts from Susan.
It was just like her...sweet and insightful.

MARRYING SUSAN MADE ME a kinder, gentler Arthur.

Almost immediately, I went from being an angry, edgy and moody (traits I owned since I was a kid) to a mellow kind of guy that even surprised me.

I was now hopefully borderline pleasant! When somebody cut me off on the highway, I didn't flip my top, step on the gas, and chase them down. I just smiled, shook my head in disbelief, and put another John Denver CD into the player.

The lifetime outdoorsmen and hunter morphed into an ecologically sensitive animal-lover. The old Arthur thought nothing of going in the woods by himself and shooting a deer. The new Arthur would see a snail struggling across the hot concrete driveway, pick it up and place it on the grass, so nobody accidentally ran it over.

There was also something else. I decided I liked being fussed over. When Susan bought me a new shirt or piece of clothing, I stopped telling her I didn't need it, save your money. Instead, I found myself saying things like, "That's great, dear. What a nice surprise. Just what I wanted, etc." I don't think I've ever met a woman who was so thoughtful in so many little ways. Eventually, however, I ran out of closet space.

~

Unfortunately, things weren't all good. I noticed the more sensitive I became, the more paranoid I became of about the potential of crippling angina attacks. These concerns led to more frequent visits to the local emergency room. God bless her heart, Susan never complained, but I sensed she was wondering where all this was going to lead? It was like we had boarded a train to some unknown destination. To be perfectly honest, it was a little scary. But we both continued to do what we had learned to do—act naturally…sort of.

I used my strange sense of humor to keep things light around the house, working in the showroom, and doing my little household projects. But I realized Susan was now watching me like a hawk.

One day we were reorganizing the family room. She wanted a table and lamp between the two couches sitting at a right angle. "No problem," I said, "I'll just extend the cord in a small conduit and run it around the corner to the closest wall outlet."

"Are you sure?" she said skeptically. "How about I test the outlet in the closet first, so this is not all for naught?"

I let her have her way. I knew she was thinking what might happen to me if the electrical source was unstable or short circuited.

Susan plugged the lamp into the closet outlet. "Works fine," she smiled and walked away. I started pushing the wire into the slit in the conduit with my hand. It got stuck, so I took a screwdriver and started jamming the wire into the conduit. I guess I cut the wire or something. The next thing I knew sparks were flying and the lights shut down. I started to get angry at myself.

Her eyes opened like an inspector general. Her body language was crystal clear. Did Arthur hurt himself? Did he rattle the old ticker unnecessarily? My odd sense of humor kicked in. "So, when did you join OSHA?" (the federal government's Occupational Safety and Health Administration).

She didn't smile. I thought to myself either she didn't get the OSHA reference or she believed she was in the middle of one of those man-woman "damned if I do and damned if I don't" things. We lite a candle. I told her eyes Thirty minutes later, the lights went back on, and the lamp worked perfectly. I smiled smugly. OSHA responded sweetly, "Arthur, I just think you need to be more careful when you're working with electricity."

I then moved the couches into the desired position. I was a little out of breath, but I didn't say anything.

~

Food monitoring also became a part of my life.

It started simply enough. "Arthur, do you think you should eat that? Arthur, doesn't that contain too much fat? Arthur, perhaps you should consider something else?"

I responded, "*Unass* me, woman." (The definition of *unass* in the Mercado Unabridged Dictionary is to get off my back).

In my heart, I knew Susan was just trying to keep me around, so I changed tactics. I began to pout like a little boy when I didn't get my way. I figured she'd melt out of sympathy. Let's just say the tactic backfired and leave it at that.

We moved to phase two of the Mercado Food Monitoring Program. I started to eat more healthy foods in the recommended portions. I started feeling better, and Susan was happier.

Things got more complicated. The health of Susan's mother in San Clemente started to deteriorate: periodic dementia, to assisted living, to a full-blown nursing home. At the same time, my angina worsened, the medications started to pile up, and I became a regular at the nearby urgent care facility. Before long, I'm forced to undergo several additional stent procedures. The pattern was the same; I would get some initial relief, and then the angina would start again.

Between working long hours, taking care of her mother, and watching me deteriorate, Susan was exhausted, but rarely complained or acted flustered.

Privately, I started to worry. Was there any chance that my heart condition could reverse itself or at least stabilize? I began to feel less and less like my old self. I wondered if she noticed me getting up in the middle of the night when I had one of those now frequent angina attacks?

I knew caring for both me and her mother had to be making her weary. I didn't know what to do. But through it all, Susan remained her calm, sensitive self. That warm, engaging smile never seemed to leave her face. It was beyond amazing. Each day began and ended the same way, with a warm smile that made me proud to call her my wife and my protector.

~

Professor "Einstein" Mercado came to another realization during the early days of our marriage. I not only enjoyed her thoughtfulness, but I also very much looked forward to getting her little surprises. I didn't say that in so many words, but she knew. (I think).

It was my birthday. Mindy, Susan, and I decided to have a quiet family celebration—just the three of us. At the restaurant, Susan pulled out a box with a gold ribbon. "Happy Birthday, this is for you."

I opened the box. Carefully wrapped in white tissue paper was a ceramic figurine—a big strong lion sat protecting a baby lamb.

"When I saw this, I knew it was perfect. It's so you."

I smiled graciously. "Thank you, so much. It's beautiful."

I had no idea what the hell she was talking about.

She explained. "The Arthur I know is strong as a lion on the outside but gentle as a lamb on the inside."

At that moment, I knew I was the luckiest man in the world.

~

During the last 20 years, Susan has taught me so much about life and about relationships. One of the most important may be that *exposing the people you love to your softer side transmits strength, not vulnerability.*

Chapter 41

Buddy

Buddy is the cutest damn canine you've ever seen.

"ARTHUR, I THOUGHT YOU MIGHT like this," said my sister Lori, handing me a scruffy ten-pound Shiatsu buried in a fluff of gold-colored hair.

It was love at first sight. He was a cute little guy with moxie. I put him down, he came right up to my ankles and started jumping. He barked just once. As I quickly learned, Buddy never barked more than once. He used to go out the door, do his business, and then bark once when he returned to let you know he was there. If you didn't hear him, he'd just sit and wait patiently until you noticed him.

I remember the expression on Susan's face that first day. She was none too pleased when I told Lori I'd be happy to take the little fella. About three days later, I took *My Dog* to get him groomed. The groomer suggested a teddy bear haircut. When Susan got home from work that day, she saw the new improved Buddy and fell in love with him. She picked him up, cuddled him and refused to put him down for an hour. I told her if she kept holding him, he was going to forget how to walk.

Buddy went everywhere with us. He was our baby. And as parents tend to do with children, we showered him with gifts and toys. He had this basket that was almost two-feet-high by two-feet-wide. When we bought him a new toy, he played with it for days until he got bored; then he'd move on.

When he wanted to play with me specifically, he'd go to his basket and dig through the toys until he got precisely the one he wanted to use. He'd leave the rest of the stuff laying around the room for Susan to clean-up. Buddy was just like having a kid who assumed it was somebody else's job to clean up his mess. That was one, spoiled dog!

While he liked all his toys, Buddy's absolute favorite was a simple, multi-colored piece of lambskin. It was not unusual to see him toss 20 toys out of his basket until he got to that damn lambskin, then he'd drag it all over the house for hours on end.

Buddy also loved chocolate. (In case you are not aware, chocolate is a no-no for dogs. They can die from consuming too much). One day Susan bought a pound of Hershey's chocolate kisses (the ones wrapped in silver foil) and put them in a bowl on the coffee table.

After coming home from work, I decided to treat myself to a few but noticed the bowl was practically empty. I assumed Susan really loved the stuff and decided to let her finish the bowl. She and I were sitting reading the papers one night. I decided to tease her, "You buy a whole bag of kisses and don't leave your husband any."

That's when we discovered she hadn't eaten even one. In fact, she assumed the disappearing bowl was my doing. The next day, I took Buddy for a walk; he decided to poop. There mixed in his poop was a pile of silver foil candy wrappers, and he wasn't feeling too good. We rushed to the vet, who informed us the dog had eaten a lot of chocolate and that we needed to be more careful. He gave us a prescription—an expensive food additive that Buddy wound up taking the rest of his life. Of course, to make sure he'd eat the damn stuff without grousing around. We discovered we had to mask the stuff in cubes of steak, pork, or chicken. He rejected cheaper meats like hot dogs and hamburgers—too ordinary, I guess.

For almost a month after the vet visit, Buddy would stand by the edge of the coffee table and sniff the empty candy dish. I'm sure he wondered what the hell happened to HIS candy. Seemed like no matter what we did that dog craved chocolate. One time, we caught him rummaging through an Easter basket full of goodies that I had bought for Susan. He had taken everything out of the basket, placed it neatly to the side until he found the chocolate eggs.

To say Buddy was spoiled would be an understatement. He had four beds, one in the family room, two in our bedroom, and one for the car—Susan decided it cruel to let the dog simply sleep in the back seat.

~

Buddy gave as well as received.

I hadn't seen Buddy for almost a month by the time I came home from the hospital after the trifecta: out-of-body experience + stroke + extensive rehab. It was like old home week. He joyfully pawed at my feet and then started hopping around like a Mexican jumping bean. It took almost 20 minutes to calm him down. It made me feel wanted. Hell, I didn't get the same welcome from Susan!

That night, when I went to sleep, I felt this pair of eyes staring at me. I woke up to find Buddy right in my face. I whispered, "Good Buddy." He then snuggled next to me and put his head on my chest. That was the beginning of a ritual that would last until Buddy died.

Buddy lived with us for over ten years. As I said earlier, he was family. When he was diagnosed with cancer and died shortly after that. I cried for days. My outpouring surprised both Susan and myself. Neither one of us had ever seen me cry so much.

In many ways, Buddy was the love of my life—after Susan and Mindy.

~

Buddy taught me a few things.

If you fall in love with somebody, brace yourself for that moment of separation. It will last a long time.

And, never enter a relationship unless you truly love somebody. Then never stop telling them you love them.

Chapter 42

Wally

Imagine falling in love with a goldfish? I did.

WALLY AND I WERE MORE than just friends: we were soulmates.

We shared similar personality traits—we both enjoyed food and were not big talkers.

We also had shared life experiences. We both had out-of-body experiences with real low odds of survival. I think that's the tie that bound us.

Unlike some friends, Wally was real low maintenance; he just liked to swim around in his fishbowl and be feed at the same time every day. The only other thing he ever wanted was clean, filtered water, which was no big deal. I'd come home from work, turn the light on in the family room, take care of his needs, tell him about my day then he'd tell me about his, and that was that.

~

One day, I walked in the door after work, and Susan gave me a kiss as she whispered softly in my ear, "We have fleas in the family room."

I flew down to the hardware store to buy one of those bug bombs. The guy behind the counter said, "It's easy to use. Just pop the cap; it releases a spray in whatever room you place it. The only thing the manufacturer suggests is to get out of the room, preferably the house, for a few hours, to let the stuff work its magic."

An hour later we released the bug bomb, and then went out for a nice romantic dinner. Afterwards, we stopped her sister and her husband's house for coffee and dessert. We were having a great time, but I kept thinking I forgot something. Ever feel that way?

We got home about 10 p.m. I headed for the family room to turn on the lights and open a few screened windows to get the treated air circulating. Suddenly, I remembered what I forgot. I had left Wally and his fishbowl in the room.

There was my buddy, floating face up in the water. He was lifeless. I was distraught. Susan said, "I think he's dead."

I knew I couldn't let my buddy die like that. I grabbed the bowl and headed to the kitchen. I fished (pardon the pun) him out of the bowl with a small strainer and told Susan to hold Wally while I changed the water. Seconds later, I put Wally back in the bowl and started swishing him around with my index finger, hoping against hope. Thirty seconds go by. Then 60. It feels like a lifetime. Crazy as this sounds, I could feel my heart racing from the excitement. Suddenly, Wally started swimming around. It was like he got a jolt of healing love. I smiled. Susan smiled. I put my face up close to the side of the fishbowl. Crisis averted.

"Go, boy, Wally. That's a good boy."

Wally and I were now soulmates forever. We both had shared an out-of-body experience. And, I learned how to administer CPR to a goldfish.

~

All's well that ends well. Usually.

In no time, Wally was back to his old self, eating, swimming, and not talking a lot. The thing was the damn pesky fleas returned. We did an instant replay with the bug bomb. This time, it was a Saturday afternoon. We went shopping to kill some time. Speaking of killing things, yup, you got it. Once again, I forgot to move Wally and his bowl.

This time, I was concerned but not flustered. After all, Susan and I now had a patented goldfish CPR process that worked. As I rushed the bowl to the kitchen, Susan handed me the strainer. Looked a little like a nurse handing the doctor a scalpel in the operating room. As she calmly held Wally in the strainer, I put fresh water in the bowl. Susan then lower Wally, strainer and all, into his bowl as she whispered, "here you go boy." I then gently stirred the water with the old index finger. It took a little longer for Wally to recover this time, but before too long, his little tail flickered.

Wally's involvement with CPR taught me a few things.

Fish or human, if you can, avoid out-of-body experiences completely. They can be traumatic.

Secondly, the more out-of-body experiences you have, the harder it is to rejoin the living.

Although I was never able to find a goldfish mortality table and projected life expectancies, Wally seemed to live a full, happy life for a goldfish. And, I made certain during our many subsequent conversations to avoid jokes about bug bombs and the afterlife.

Wally subsequently died of natural causes about two years later. When he passed, I gave him a proper friend's funeral. I put him in this little wooden box and buried him in the flower garden. It was a pretty and peaceful spot.

To this day, Wally's fishbowl, filled with a few artifical flowers, sits in in the family room, as a kind of memorial.

Chapter 43

Murphy

This is my buddy Murphy, shy, reserved, but always cool,
like someone I know real well!

HAPPY WIFE, HAPPY LIFE. Corny but true.

It turned out Susan loved cats. So, it was not surprising we added a cat to our family. Interesting change of pace after a monkey, a goldfish, a lion, and a lamb.

We decided to name him after a friend of mine, Jim Murphy. Jim was in the car business, had a bad heart, and had overcome a few of life's little obstacles: a five-bypass, an massive endarterectomy, and two knee replacement surgeries.

Didn't take long to realize we had bought a very shy cat. When people visited, Murphy darted upstairs and hid in the bedroom. Like clockwork, when people left he came back downstairs.

Like Wally, and unlike that pain-in-the-ass Peppi, Murphy was really low-maintenance. Just a bit of extra food and a little love, and he was good to go.

Like Buddy, Murphy had a distinct evening ritual. Since they co-existed for a number of years, I wondered if that was where he developed his habit.

About four in the morning, Murphy would crawl into bed with me, sit on my chest, and begin to stare and purr. He wouldn't stop purring until I woke up. Then he'd gently butt his head into my chin. I'd pet him, say "good boy," and then he'd roll over and go back to sleep.

Susan always smiled.

~

Like Wally, Murphy loved to play. He was like the son I never had.

He particularly enjoyed laser-mouse tag. I bought this thing that looks like a wireless remote at the pet store. When I turned it on, it emitted a red beam, not unlike a presentation pointer. Sometimes, I'd flash the beam up and down the stairs for fun. Murphy would go crazy and start zooming around the bed like a maniac. When he finally tired, he preferred the peace and quiet of the pantry closet. He would lay on a plastic bag that made a crunching sound and cover himself with a double brown paper bag that sat in the corner. He could sleep for hours.

When I was in the hospital—who knows which time —they gave me a soft ball with a smiley face that laughed when you squeezed it. I thought it was silly, but when I came home, I discovered Murphy loved the damn thing. He would push it around every room in the house. When he finished, he just stopped and purred. It was Murphy's way of communicating he didn't take himself too seriously. With each passing life incident I realize the best way to handle things is the Murphy way: *Try not to take everything seriously, just kick the ball around the house as long as you can.*

~

Murphy could also be a sulker.

One time, Susan and I went to the desert on a four-day vacation. I was between stent procedures. I've learned you gotta make hay when the sun shines. When we returned, it was clear the cat was so pissed we didn't bring him along he wouldn't let us touch him for days. I fixed his ass. I wouldn't give him his smiley face. It was like a

Mexican standoff. But I never raised my hand or voice. Eventually, we agreed to disagree, and the matter was forgotten!

I've changed a lot since the good old days of beating the shit out of Spanky and killing deer. I don't think I could harm a butterfly anymore, much less my buddy Murphy. That brings me to another life lesson, compliments of Murphy: *animals are living creatures that can teach you how to be a more sensitive, caring person than you ever thought possible.*

Part Four

Bumpy Road Ahead

Chapter 44

Warranty's Up

Pre(left) and Post (right) Stent X-Rays.
Note the broken wire in my chest.

TIME PASSED, we were a close family of six: Susan, myself, Wally, the Lion, the Lamb and Buddy. We all lived in a nice, two-story house in Chino Hills, south of Los Angeles, but, like always, there were a few issues.

My best friend Bill called. He'd found a great high-income job selling Cadillacs in San Diego County. He wanted me to go south to join him. I take the job but initially decide to stay in Chino Hills. Eventually, the two-hour commute started to take its toll. I was tired all the time. So, I began to stay with Bill and his wife and commuted home every other night.

I also started to realize our neighborhood was changing for the worse. And Susan concern about person safety had left her with a smaller and smaller circle of friends. So, in January 1998 decided to move to booming San Diego. We figured I'd have no trouble transferring my sales skills to another car dealership, Cadillac or otherwise, and Susan's impressive academic and professional resume, would offer her numerous job opportunities. she'll have

Before long, we found ourselves loving downtown San Diego and its surrounding eateries: fish nibbles at the take-out window next to Anthony's Fish House on the

Embarcadero; mouthwatering breaded swordfish at the
Brigantine Restaurant on Point Loma; and decadent
desserts at our new favorite neighborhood restaurant, the
Elephant Bar.

~

Deep down own, I knew my health continued to
deteriorate. The warranty on my five by-pass was just
about up! Like every middle-aged man in denial about his
mortality, I just ignored the new signals. I figured why the
hell spend the time in a hospital when there were places
to go, things to see, and people to meet. I thought, what's
a little angina? It always seemed to pass.

One night, we're sitting at home, and my stomach
began to ache something fierce. Susan hustled me into
the car for a visit to the emergency room. I told her to
"hurry," to run the red lights before I blacked out. I
wound up spending three days at the hospital. The
doctors did all kinds of tests and gave me a host of IVs.
The diagnosis was better than expected: a stubborn
stomach infection that took multiple antibiotics to kill.

The following week, I visited my GP with Susan for a
routine follow-up. The GP strongly suggested I see a
cardiologist. A few days later, I visited my new
cardiologist. I tell him, my main goal is "to do what I
have to do to get more mileage out of this aging Model-T
body."

He laughed then checked my vitals. His recommendation
surprised me. "Eliminate all medications and replace them
with a single water pill." I thought to myself, *are you sure?*
The doctor didn't look like he was in the mood to be
challenged, so I keep my mouth shut.

~

Saturday morning, Susan and I were food shopping. I
felt my heart racing. The store had one of those blood
pressure machines. The top-line was over 200. I called the
cardiologist's office. He was gone for the weekend. We
headed straight for the Urgent Care Center at Scripps
Rancho Bernardo, not far from the store.

The doctor on duty took my vitals. Still off the charts. My blood pressure was now 215/115, and my pulse was 115 lying down. *She* asked if I had made any recent changes in my meds. I explained what had happened. She strongly suggested I return to my prior prescription regimen until "matters were sorted out." That's medical doubletalk for "somebody made a mistake." The nurse then gave me a few medications and asked me to lie down until the meds took effect. About two hours later, all my vitals were back to normal, and Susan drove us home.

By Sunday, I was feeling a little better. I decided two things: to tell my cardiologist he's done and to begin an accelerated search for a *female* cardiologist.

Why a female?

Four reasons:

1. They listen to what the patient has to say.
2. They're more cautious about abrupt changes.
3. They're not afraid to answer questions.
4. I'm more comfortable talking to a female doctor.

(I've always wondered why I find it so easy to talk to women about personal things. I guess I blame that on the way Pop raised me. As I said earlier, he never hugged me or showed overt affection, except that one time when he was certain they were going to ship me to Vietnam).

~

Susan and I spent the weekend researching cardiologists. All roads seemed to lead to a doctor by the name of Mimi Guarneri, founder and medical director at a place called the Scripps Integrative Center in La Jolla. She had nothing but rave patient reviews. I figured I'd make an appointment in due time. But, the week didn't start well. I had severe chest pains.

Mimi agreed to see me immediately. Next thing I knew, I was sitting in front of this passionate, waif-like doctor who had already reviewed my medical records. She listened to my story. She then started talking about how the center blended allopathic care with evidence-based complementary treatments and therapies. I didn't have a clue what the hell she was talking about. But, I'm an instinctive sort of person, and I was confident she was the right cardiologist for me: smart, caring, kind, sensitive, and a great listener.

After she had examined me, she told me she was concerned about my condition. I smiled and said, "so am I." She scheduled a stress test for the next day. The test had to be aborted in midstream because my blood pressure was too high. That led to a nuclear stress test, which is a chemical stress test where the doctor looks for potential arterial blockages by tracking dyes injected into your arteries. The test doesn't hurt, but it sure makes you feel weird.

"Arthur," she said, "we need to do an angiogram. Despite your prior five bypass, I'm certain you have a significant blockage in so-and-so artery, and you'll need one, maybe two. Depends"

I raised my eye brows. "Depends on what?"

"Arthur," she said confidently, "no need to worry, we do these procedures every day. There is less than a 3 percent chance of complications."

Right then and there, I realized the warranty on my five by-pass had worn out. When they wheeled me into the Cath Lab, I was worried. Big, tough Artie was worried. I was wide awake as the dye goes was inserted into my arteries. Even though it was eight years ago, my mind clearly imagined the wall with the window and the two guys watching intently.

When I woke, I discovered there actually were two guys watching Mimi. She called them her "complications crew." Their role: to do whatever in case something went amiss. Fortunately, there was no need. The entire procedure was just over an hour. Not bad given my doomsday expectations.

Of course, I had no idea at the time that I was going to become an honorary member of the "frequent visitor club."

~

Things changed drastically after that stent procedure. (More about that later). But just seeing those guys that day made me ask myself some heavy questions.

Is all the stuff we obsess over really that important? Would I even spend a minute on the subject if I knew this was your last day on earth?

This latest cardiac procedure also provided another insight.

if you simply must have a stent procedure, surround yourself with beautiful nurses. It's a lot more fun!

Chapter 45

Out-of-Body

Doctor Mimi Guarneri long-time keeper of her unusually resilient, but high-maintenance patient.

I'M NOW A Doctor Guarneri Regular.

She checked my condition about every 90 days. Thanks to her wonderful care and attention, I felt pretty good despite my little ups and downs.

"Hmmm," she said as she listened to the blood pumping through my carotid arteries.

"Arthur, we may have a problem. It sounds like there may be some blood flow restrictions." I didn't like the way she stared at me with those big dark eyes. "Arthur, we need to do some more tests right now!" Minutes later, the tests are scheduled. I just keep my mouth shut and go, although I do remember thinking, *no matter what the hell it is, I can handle it.*

They took a sonogram of my carotid arteries. The doctor began spouting the kind of news I didn't want to hear "Arthur, one of your arteries has a 50 percent blockage, which is bad, but the other has an 85 percent blockage. If we don't get that artery cleaned out quickly, so the blood flow increases, you could suffer a massive stroke and be paralyzed for life."

I don't want to bore everybody with the surgical details. Suffice to say; we did an endarterectomy. They placed two clamps on the artery about three inches apart then opened and cleaned the artery. The surgery was declared an immediate success. Miraculously, the blockage in the other artery was also dramatically reduced. The doctor assumed that clearing the one artery created an increased blood flow which had a direct impact on the other.

I was still in a sort of twilight from the anesthesia when I was wheeled into a room in the critical care unit. At that point, no one realized a clot had found its way to my brain.

The next two days were lost somewhere in time. I had suffered a stroke. I was lying in bed, lifeless. I knew there was something wrong, but I was "borderline stupidville" from all the drugs.

~

What happened next remains quite vivid years later.

The bed rails were up, and I'm connected to a host of IV tubes. Suddenly, I'm standing in the corner of the room looking at my body on the floor. I look back at the bed.

I notice the safety rails are up, and the IV bags are lying on the floor next to a body. All the colors are very clear and bright. I turn my head to the corner of the room where I had been standing to see if I was still there. There was only emptiness. My body wasn't there.

It was the weirdest feeling I've ever experienced.

I turned and looked straight ahead. There are at least ten people running toward me from the other end of the room.

Next thing I know, I woke up in bed with Dr. Guarinari standing over me. "We found you on the floor. You appear to have crawled out of bed." I explained what had transpired. She asked me to sit up. I couldn't. I was paralyzed on my right side, had no use of my right leg and very little use of my right arm.

Dr. Guarneri offered the only other possibility she knew of. "Sounds like you may have had an out-of-body experience."

"An out-of-body what?"

"You died for a few minutes. But the good news is that you're back."

I was stunned and shaken.

Dr. Guarneri knew we were beyond traditional medical science. For starters, she recommended that two healing-touch practitioners pray over me.

"No problem," I mumbled before returning to a semi-conscious state. I'm told I was in-and-out of consciousness for the next few days. But, I clearly felt the healers' presence clearly in my mind.

~

I was moved to another area in the hospital to better prepare me for my return home. We had this ritual. The nurses propped me up in bed. Since I had no control over my right arms, legs, or body, I would fall over. They would smile and pick me up, and we'd try again. After falling like a rag doll a few more times, I would get real irritated.

It was now certain. I had suffered a mini-stroke during the surgery, which caused both the out-of-body experience and my partial paralysis. As the doctor explained, we missed it the first time because the incidence of stroke after your procedure is very low.

"How low," I asked out of curiosity.

"Two in 100, maybe less."

I thought to myself, *how come I never win the long shots when I gamble!*

~

A few days later, during one of Susan's visits, we walked past the room where I had the out-of-body experience. I was amazed; the room was tiny. There was hardly room for 3 or 4 people, much less 10 people walking across the room.

Chapter 46

Dart Board

When you've had a stroke, playing darts can be hard work.

A WEEK AFTER THE endarterectomy and my out-of-body experience, Dr. Guarneri told me my vital signs had stabilized, and I needed to be admitted to a hospital that specialized in stroke-rehabilitation.

I was concerned about another change. Another potential mishap. I asked, "Do I really have too? Maybe I can do without." The answer was like the offer you couldn't refuse. "Mr. Mercado, think of the rehab sessions as a bonus program that comes free with the endarterectomy."

I was plain scared. No bravado this time. I went quietly. An ambulance took me to Scripps Memorial Hospital in Encinitas. When I arrived, they put me in a wheelchair. While I had come to accept the reality that I was paralyzed and might need a wheelchair for the moment, I had no intention of lying down and giving up.

My entire life had followed a pattern. *When I'm pushed to the wall, I dig down deep and bring up whatever is necessary to overcome life's latest obstacle.*

~

The first few days seemed to be filled with silly therapy exercises. But I was a good boy and did what I was told. Then came "the day at the darts" as I jokingly called the event sometime later. The therapist asked a group of us to throw darts. Since I was always good at darts, I volunteered to go first. After all, I had been through, so I decided to do a little showing off.

"Are you sure you want to go first? Arthur, perhaps…"

I interrupted, "Piece of cake."

The dart board was only about eight feet from where we were gathered. I threw the first dart; it landed about four feet in front of me. I couldn't believe it. They gave me another dart. This time I threw it super hard; again, it landed about four feet from me. I was incredulous, but I started to get the message. Something was seriously wrong. They gave me one more chance. I took the dart, more determined than ever. I put my entire body into the throw. The same thing happened.

I finally got it. Even though I had regained some use of my right arm, it was still too weak to use it consistently, reliably. That was the last time I questioned anything those caring people asked me to do.

~

For one of the few times in my life, I became a little depressed. You know, stuff like, Why me? What next? But I wasn't outwardly negative; I didn't want anybody to think big Art's boy was a whiner. But I needed support.

Fortunately, my brother-in-law, Joe, an active Martine Colonel, came to visit me every evening while I was in the hospital. He was witty, inspirational, and motivating. He always had a joke or some kind words. During one visit, he told me he had never seen Susan so happy. I'm thinking to myself, *I've caused Susan nothing but worry and concern, and she couldn't be happier?*

Susan also came to see me every day after she got off work. My room had this window that I could see out but nobody could see in. One day, I watched Susan walk up to the hospital from the parking lot. She had the saddest, stressed look on her face. I knew I was the cause. I felt so guilty.

By the time she came into my room, she had her usual big smile, like everything was great. "How is my favorite husband today?" I knew then and there I had to do whatever it took to walk out of that hospital. I called in my therapist. I told her how sad Susan looked when she walked in.

"Love has a way of doing that," she said. That's when I knew *I was going to regain complete mobility because I had people who loved me.*

I said, "Let's get me. And, I want to leave this joint on my terms. No wheelchair, no walker, not even a cane."

The therapist saw the determination in my eyes. "Well then, we've got work to do." By the end of the second week, I was helping the other patients to walk and cheering people up in the halls. They told me I was a positive role model for the other patients. I had no idea what they were talking about. All I knew was that *fierce determination could overcome a hell of a lot of obstacles.*

~

Finally, I was home-ready!

Before I left Scripps, they asked if they could take my picture. I asked why. They said they wanted to put it on the cover of their new brochure. I thought they were crazy. They thought my recovery will an inspiration to others. So I did it, but unfortunately never kept a copy.

My forced vacation was over. It was time go back to selling Cadillacs on the showroom floor. When I walked in the door, everybody stared at me, like I was going to drop dead, there and then.

I told everybody to lighten up. I went out and sold more cars that week than anybody else. In fact, I sold so many cars that I won the annual sales contest and a trip to a round of celebrity golf.

As you're probably aware, selling cars is a competitive job. I guess that's why it's called a "cutthroat career." But, when my name was posted as the winner, there was no jealousy, no complaining, just a ton of "way to goes." In fact, from that week on, the dealership became a kinder, gentler place. I don't know why...*Maybe just knowing somebody died and came back to life makes people friendlier.*

Chapter 47
Papa Does Golf

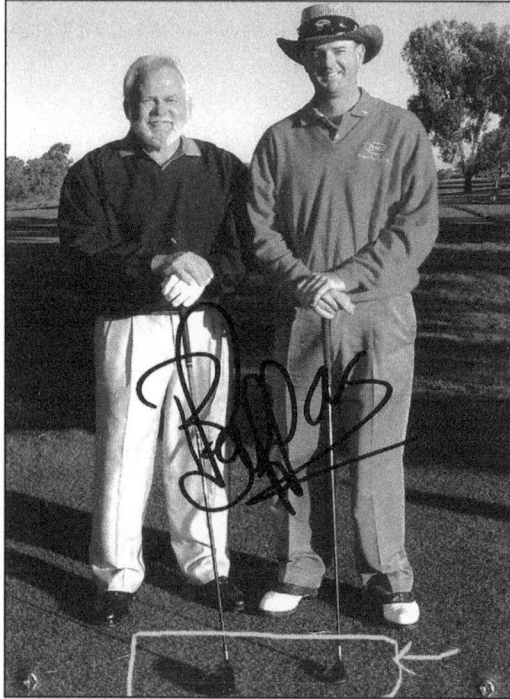

Golf Pro, Brendan Pappas, and I
switch golf clubs to make me look good.

AFTER RAISING MINDY solo and marrying Susan, the greatest event of my life was playing in the Buick Invitational Pro-Am with golf pro, Brendan Pappas, at the world-famous Torrey Pines Golf Course in La Jolla, California.

After I had given up hunting, golf had become my sport. I just loved it. I wasn't great, but with a 25 handicap, I could hold my own with most of my friends.

The management at our Cadillac dealership announced the company was running a killer sales contest: the top salesman during the next quarter would get to play in a foursome with an honest-to-goodness pro at the Pro-Am. I loved the prize but didn't think I had a shot at winning. Our place was filled with so many experienced luxury car salesmen.

But I worked like a man possessed. I closed everyone that walked in, I ran a referral drive, and I just made a ton of cold calls. I started out at the top of the leader board and stayed there for the entire 12-week period. The contest results were announced in front of everybody. Peer envy was mixed with polite applause. The buzz around the water cooler was how this low-key, soft-spoken dude could reach the top of the leader board. Never told the other salesmen my secret sauce—old fashioned honesty. I just treated everybody the way I would want to be treated. Customers respected that.

~

Winning was one thing; playing in the foursome was another.

First, there was my two-week-old torn rotator cuff, which might make it difficult to swing but unlikely to make my 25 handicap any worse. Hell, I figured, even if my rotator cuff hurt like the devil, I should be able to finish the 18 holes. After all, when would I get another chance like this? Besides, when seven-handicap Kevin, the most aristocratic salesman in the office, volunteered to be my caddy, how could I possibly say no?

That left me with obstacle number two. I hadn't been feeling well due to frequent loss of breath, pains in my chest, etc. About a week before I was supposed to collect my prize, my doctor told me I needed another angiogram. His comforting thought. "Once we get in there, we'll have a better idea of what we need to do."

The procedure went smoothly. After regaining consciousness, I learned, "We had to insert a few more stents to keep your blood flowing properly."

"How long will I be laid up?" I asked.

"A week, maybe two. Depends."

"Depends on what?"

"How fast you heal," replied Dr. Guarneri. I explained I had to heal super-fast because I was playing in the Pro-Amat Torrey Pines the following Saturday.

"Arthur, you may have to shelve that one," she smiled.

I thought to myself, *not a chance. She doesn't understand the determination of one Arthur Mercado.*

~

The Torrey Pines course was beautiful that Wednesday morning. Perfectly groomed green carpet, not a cloud in the sky, and birds chirping so loud they drowned out the warning from my doctor that "I was playing against her better judgment." All the fuss at the doctor's office didn't rattle me one bit. I was shaky but still on cloud nine.

When I arrived at the course, I found out part of the prize was to get fitted for a professional set of golf attire. Thirty minutes later, I'm at the driving range in my Ben Hogan slacks and shirt and brand new rubber-cleated Foot-Joys. I took out my favorite club, a five-wood, which usually allowed me to get the ball in the air and hit it a reasonable distance with some consistency. I looked to my right; I was standing next to John Daly. I gulped and shanked the ball 70 yards, tops. I kept my head down and teed up another shot. Another shank. I looked at the guy waiting for me to finish so that he can take a few swings. It was Phil Mickelson. I tried to mask my ineptness by taking a few practice swings. I noticed he wasn't offering any free advice, so I nodded and headed to the putting green.

A few minutes later, I stepped to the first tee. There I'm introduced to my partner for the day, this big tall dude, Brendan Pappas, a regular on the PGA tour. I had only one thought; God I hope he doesn't talk to Daly or Mickelson before we get started. Brendan walked over and extended his hand. "Hello, Arthur. Great day for a round of golf, isn't it?" I smiled. I was a little intimidated.

The starter announced over the microphone, "Next on the tee, Arthur Mercado from San Diego." Brendan got out of the way. My heart started to race. I imagined a thousand eyes watching me. I mumbled to myself, "God, I hope I don't kill somebody." After a few practice swings, I hit the ball straight down the fairway. About 80 yards.

"Well, it's on the fairway," said Brendan trying to be positive. The caddy handed Brendan a driver with a head the size of a Valencia eating orange. The ball went 275 maybe 280 yards.

Brendan asked me as we walked, "What's your handicap?"

"*About* 25," I responded nervously.

He smiled. I could see he wondered how close to 25 was *about*. "Arthur, I think the max we can put down is 21. That okay with you?" I nodded.

It turned out he was the nicest guy. He made me feel totally at ease. "Mind if I give you a little tip?" said Brendan. "Next time, why don't you just bring your feet a little closer together? May give you a little more distance and direction." I took his advice. The rest of the hole didn't go so badly. I wound up with a triple-bogey.

The next tee was loaded with photographers and equipment. It was time for souvenir pictures. I'm delighted. I needed a break to gather my emotions.

There I was: Me with Brendan Pappas at the second hole at Torrey Pines. My memento for the ages! The photographer positioned us on the tee with drivers in hand. He measured the light, then snapped. "Done, gentlemen."

Brendan paused and said, "Sorry, we need one more." Then he looked at me and pointed. "What's that thing in your hand?" I looked at my club. I'm holding my favorite five-wood. It looks like a pea next to his driver.

"Arthur, you don't want your wife to see you in a picture with that little stick."

Brendan handed me his oversized driver with an extended custom shaft because of his height. He took my five-wood. If you look closely at the drivers in the picture at the front of this chapter, you'll notice the difference in the size of the club heads. Thank you, Brendan!

After the photo shoot, I began to play a lot better. We did a lot of chit-chatting about golf and life. He explained professional golf was a tough way to make a living because so much of it was mental. I joked that playing with a torn rotator cuff and a few recently inserted stents also had its mental challenges. He was horrified but cool. As we played each ensuing hole, Brendan watched my every move. By the tenth hole, he was completely relaxed—after all, I had shown no immediate signs of dropping dead!

When we finished, we tallied up the cards. I shot 104, which was respectable, given we were playing a pro-level course with narrow fairways, thick rough and greens so fast you felt like you were putting on tiles. Of course, Brendan shot a bit lower! I asked to see his score. He just said he couldn't win the open with it. We left things at that.

That evening, my chest and shoulders were sore. I guess you should assume if you're going to play 18 holes of golf with a torn rotator cuff and a few new stents in the old arteries, there may be a little post-play discomfort.

I know what you're wondering. The stents held. No post procedure emergency room visit.

The best thing about golf to me? Kicking the crap out of a bunch of helpless little white balls is an emotionally gratifying experience!

Chapter 48

Two Triple-Triples

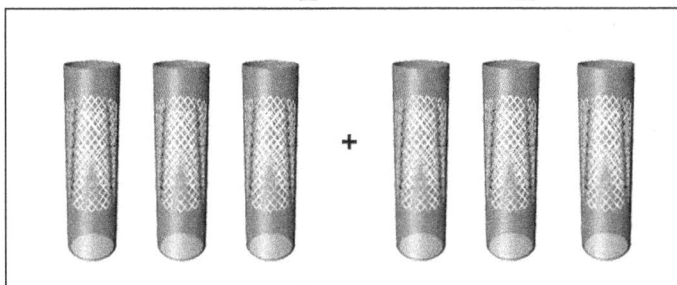

Multiple stents inclusions become my new norm.

IT WAS NOW EARLY 2002. I'd been pain-free for 18 months. I concluded *having a pain-free heart was almost as good as having a banana split with fresh whipped cream.*

But 2002 was not a very good year. I underwent angioplasties # 2, 3, 4, had stents # 3, 4, 5 inserted and received 28 minutes of intracoronary radiation.

On the positive side, Dr. G personally referred me to interventional cardiologist Dr. Paul Tierstein, whom she described as "the best stent man" in Southern California. Dr. Teirstein's "MO" was that he did nothing but stents. The way she described Dr. Tierstein, all I could think of was the In-N-Out burger advertising slogan, "The Double-Double. Two fresh hamburger patties in one roll. It's all we do!"

As it turned out, Dr. T. was a heck of a nice guy. In my first pre-op interview, I told him I sold luxury cars for a living. I pitched him on the features and benefits of the Lexus, which is what I was selling at the time. He nodded. I don't know if he ever bought one or was just picking my brain.

Somewhere in the middle of our discussion came the "good news." The good doctor explained, "Coated stents are close to receiving final FDA approval. Tests indicate they reduce scaring around stents, which allows us to use additional stents with little concern about internal complications." I think to myself *Whoopee!*

As it turned out, each 2002 procedure had its own idiosyncrasy (not "complication"). The May procedure was certainly the most memorable. My angiogram indicated I had a large stretch of blocked artery behind the heart. Too large, in fact, for a single stent or even a double. So, Dr. T. created a special triple-stent.

I'm still not sure what the most unusual part of the day was. The procedure itself or the fact that I had forgotten to sign the medical consent forms while being prepped. The hospital anti-liability patrol had me sign the papers as they wheeled the gurney down the hall into the operating theater.

~

After five stents (and counting), the endarterectomy, an out-of-body experience, and a mini-stroke, life started to get weird.

I was still trying to live a normal life—whatever that meant—but the thought of "what's next" was always in the back of my mind.

I'd done enough of these heart procedures, that I understood the process: First there was the "Pain Arrived Stage." Increased pressure in the chest, usually after exertion...like walking 50 yards up an incline. I usually performed damage control by stopping to rest. If I continued to walk—say another 100 yards—it usually required a nitro pill. Those suckers opened the arteries, lowered the pain pressure.

Sometimes, these initial angina attacks would wake me from a deep sleep. So, I'd pop a nitro or two. If the angina subsided, I would ignore it and go back to sleep. If the pain persisted, I'd visit Paul (we were now on a first name basis).

Phase Two was a little different. I called it the "Procedure Ready" phase. It examination suggested the problem was more pronounced (in doctor speak: required an intervention), I would obtain the required insurance approvals, then schedule an exploratory visit to the Cath Lab. To make the time pass between doctor visit-insurance approval-Cath Lab, I'd make more multi-song music CD's with Susan. Sometimes, I'd take out my collection of vintage baseball cards, and reshuffle their order.

Phase Three, "Just Doing It." Sometimes uncomfortable, sometimes not. Usually an angiogram, followed by an angioplasty (ultimately I had about a dozen of those), and then the catheter (tube with a hole) up the groin to the damaged artery around the heart. Ugh.

~

Susan morphed into the "diet warden." Susan was determined to reduce my odds of return visits by removing stuff that could clog my arteries.

Triple-decker BLT sandwiches were out; tofu cheese sandwiches with fake mayonnaise were in. She tried to convince me they didn't taste so bad. I nodded pleasantly. What the hell! If she was happy, I was happy. That's all that mattered. Still does.

One Thanksgiving, she decided to mix things up a bit. The aroma of a delicious beef-roast basted in its own juices filled the house. I am "authorized" a portion about the size of a silver dollar with a heaping side of vegetables steeped in the juices. My Thanksgiving turkey dinner was 97 percent fat-free.

The man who once loved one-pound burritos had been brainwashed to believe a tofu sandwich was better than sex.

~

Thankfully, 2002 finally ended. I called it the year of the *triple-triple* (three angioplasties, three stents). It was also the year I stopped denying my real situation. I stopped joking, "God gave me a strong heart and stubborn will to accept and survive my roller-coaster ride." I realized I was on borrowed time, and that each procedure was designed to give me a little breathing room (pardon the pun). But, most of all, I felt bad for Susan, a wonderful woman who hadn't sign up for all this madness.

Something Pop said a long time ago regularly reverberated in my ear. *"God is not in the business of giving a man more than he can handle. So, if you don't figure out how to work around it, the fault lies with you, not Him."*

Chapter 49

Medicine Man

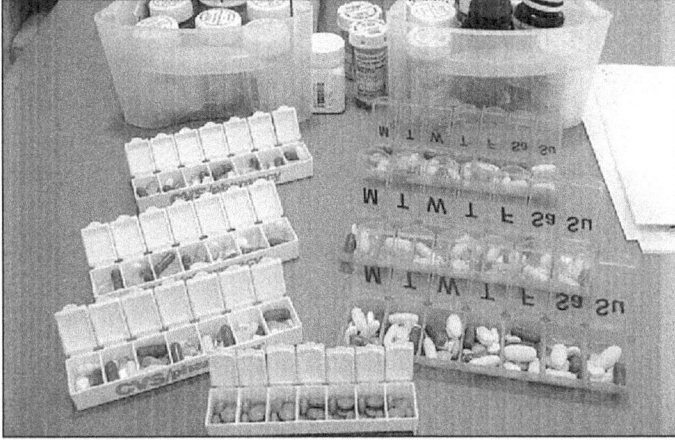

Organizing a three-week supply of 23+ medications
requires precise planning and a little bit of luck.

MY MEDICAL FILE continued to expand over the next few years. One open-heart five bypass, 13 stents (coated and uncoated), five angioplasties, one endarterectomy, two mini-strokes, 28 radiation treatments, and daily nitro patches and pills. Plus, I'm up to 23 different prescriptions a day (give or take one).

Offsetting those little annoyances is the support of great friends, a loving family, and my bizarre sense of humor. In other words, I've got "some version" of good health, to paraphrase Jack Nicholson in that wonderful movie *Something's Gotta Give*.

I also created a Mercado daily routine. First, I wake up. That always made me feel good! Then, I cranked up my computer to update my latest prescription list which now included Norvasc, Toprol-XL, Lisinopril, Aspirin, Folbic, Plavix, Crestor, Zetia, Lovaza, Protonix, Stalevo, Azilect, D-1000, Co Q-10, Nitro pills and Nitro Patches, among other stuff I can't remember now. My Excel spreadsheet (a little tough to learn for a non-techie like me) summarized what these things were, when to take what, dosage amounts, and subtleties such as before or after meals, potential side effects, etc.

Next step was turning the spreadsheet into a reality kit. I made two piles. The ones that went in the red box were morning pills; the white box was evening pills; and the plastic bag contained the five pills which make me sick to my stomach. My patented separate-and-stack process usually required two to three hours, depending upon how depressed it made me feel.

There were also few tablets that I require splitting, so I bought one of those pill splitters. But, I noticed I was starting to get the shakes which has caused me to miss the split mark and I'd wind up with a bunch of pill bits and pieces. That has led to another Mercado work-around. Unfortunately, it does make Susan grimace. I take a sharp knife, place it on the split seam and then start hitting the top of the blade with my hand. Susan's pained expression has often made me wonder how she would have reacted to watching me skin a deer in my garage, way back when?

~

Recently, Dr. G suggested I add some holistic activities to my daily routine. I tried to figure out how to meditate. When I meditated, all I could visualize was blood pressure readings. When I listened to CD's I kept hearing the Statler Brothers singing country and western standards.

Fortunately, I've found a way to fill my spare time. I completed a never-ending stream of insurance forms and disability claims. And, to keep my heart rate at or above norms, I expressed my frustration about bureaucratic delays, lost paperwork, and an endless stream of nameless, faceless people on the other end of the phone. (Despite being a lifetime democratic, I became convinced the government should play a smaller and smaller role in citizen healthcare. Gotta be cheaper and more efficient.)

~

A recent exam indicated I now have early stage Parkinson's (which means I have lots yet to come). So, we have added a few more goodies in the morning before breakfast. The pills make me nauseous, but the increased intestinal activity does stimulate my bowel movements. (Unfortunately, food doesn't taste quite as good when you're sick to your stomach).

I also now certain there is absolutely no sense complaining. *Dealing with your doctor is like being happily married. Just keep my mouth shut and do what you're asked.*

~

Parkinson's has some great positives. It's a great talking point with the ladies. If anybody asks me what's going on, I just respond, "You've got me all shook up."

Another positive: my newspaper shakes in my hand and makes the type a bit blurry when I try to read a story. I'm convinced it was like doing a daily ocular exercise: my vision has improved and eyes don't get tired as fast!

There is this one little problem with the Parkinson's. The warning labels on my latest prescriptions suggest I need to avoid things like chocolate, cheese, and tofu among other things. When I tally up all the foods that interact with all my medications, there's not much left to eat, good or bad. I'm considering the addition of tree bark to my diet! Not sure about how to season and barbecue the stuff, but I figure I there must be another work-around.

(Just looked out my living room window. The bark on my neighbor's tree looks a lot tastier than my craggy bark. When the moment presents itself, I'll ask him if he minds me harvesting some of his bark. I'm thinking about mixing the two, like a health salad).

~

After breakfast these days, I have about four hours of "good time," then I start to get a little tired. I usually take a nap to regain some energy by the time Susan gets home from work. The power nap also provides the extra burst of energy I need to take all my afternoon and evening pills.

My routine has been fine until I meet this guy Matt. He kept hassling me to tell people more about my life. He's killed my afternoons! I don't have the time to feel sorry for myself. It really pisses me off.

I've also think I've found something else to add to my daily routine. The other night I was reading this book about a Sioux Indian medicine man, Chief Running Bear. He insisted chanting improved well-being.

So, tried the Chief's "two-spirit chant." A few days into my Indian chants, the phone rang. My neighbor, who fully understood my health status, made the kindest offer. "I know Susan works, so we'll keep a listen, in case you need to get to the doctor." That was the end of the Chief's chant. (Probably for the best. I don't think there is any reliable medical research on the about the potential side effects of mixing chants and medications).

Chapter 50

Just Say Thank You

*My "new, forever" buddies (l to r) Matt, Keith, me, Kris
at our labyrinth.*

DESPITE ALL THE LOVE, medications, dieting, and good intentions, my health continued to deteriorate.

At work, prospective customers had to help me up from my desk to show them a car, and I couldn't walk more than 100 yards without the need for a nitro pill.

I finally agreed to take Dr. G's advice seriously. I enrolled in a 12-week Scripps Hospital Healing Heart program run by the doctor. It sounded like a bunch of mumbo-jumbo, but I figured, what the hell, how many other options does this tired body have? And, despite life's little setbacks, I still liked living more than the alternative.

I quickly became immersed in yoga and belly breathing, cooking and nutrition, music and stress reduction. But most of all, I learned about myself in the group support sessions.

As Matt said at the beginning of this book, I wasn't much of a talker. By the time the 12 weeks were up, they couldn't shut me up. For some inexplicable reason, I wanted to share everything. I don't know if it was the chemistry in that room or if it was just that time. I sensed it was more the former.

I also wondered after this 12-week immersion, how was I going to fill my days?

Everything in my life never seemed like much of a big deal. I always just dealt with the cards I've been handed. *I've always assumed that somebody, somewhere, was worse off, so why complain? Nobody wants to hear.*

~

Twelve weeks went by in the blink of an eye. Ozzie, the Scripps program facilitator, signaled that program was about to end. I had graduated. I felt a frightening finality. An important page of my life was about to be turned. Ozzie asked the group to form a circle, join hands, and offer Arthur Godspeed on the rest of his trip "in whatever words they felt appropriate." I was taken back by the request. I never imagined anyone would do such a thing. But I was pleased.

Two of the group's newest members, David and Roy, said something about how personally rewarding it had been to have met me. Their sentiments seemed genuine although I wasn't exactly sure what they meant. But, what happened next has changed me forever. Six eyes (Keith, Kris, and Matt) stared into my soul. To say I felt self-consciousness would be an understatement of mammoth proportions. Tough-as-nails Keith, who reminded me a lot of myself when I was younger, turned teddy bear. He called me "his rock."

"Arthur," continued Keith, "I'm far from perfect, but I've always tried to play it straight. I'm certain I'll be a better man for just knowing you. I've listened these past weeks to how you've dealt with life's difficulties. You've inspired me. You've helped me put my trivial problems in perspective. You've turned my anger, my frustration, into love. I sincerely hope you beat all the doubters and live another hundred years."

Kris, who we jokingly nicknamed Botox Bob, because of the injections he self-administered every day to function a normal life, took my breath away. "Arthur, I grew up in a family where the kids were taken for granted. The primary agenda was their agenda. So, naturally, I've always been a little cynical about the positive influence of a parent on a child. But listening to you speak about Mindy, how much you love her, and the importance you have placed on being a good parent has inspired me. I want to be a better parent. I want to give unconditional love. From now on, when I hit the inevitable bump in the parental road, I'll ask myself what would Arthur do in this situation?"

Kris touched me deeply. I cried…inside. (I have never been able to cry aloud).

The door opened, and in walked Gleneva (a prior graduate of the Healing Heart course) with a carrot cake. "Arthur, since you missed the cooking class on how to bake a low-carb, high-protein carrot cake, I have made you one as a graduation presentation."

Moments later, everyone in the room ate the carrot cake. Funny thing, the damn thing was delicious!

It was close to that time. I realized the one guy who hadn't said anything was the guy who always had something to say. The guy who continually tricked me into speaking first at every group session.

"So, Matt, what's the story?"

I said nothing more. He knew what I meant. All the eyes in the room stared at him. This guy who was so articulate, so funny, for so many weeks, seemed hard pressed to let the words go. He looked into my eyes.

"Arthur," he whispered. "It's all been said—except perhaps that I want you to know you are my role model, my hero, my friend. And, I love you."

I noticed a few tears slither down his cheek.

I looked at Ozzie.

"I don't know what to say," I mumbled.

Ozzie smiled. *"Just say thank you."*

Chapter 51

Endeavor to Persevere

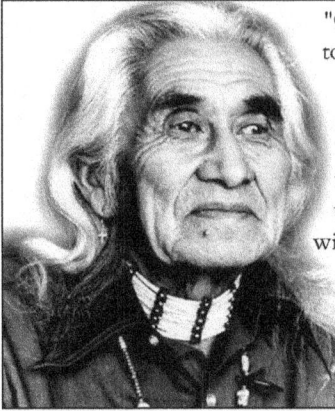

"One thing to remember is to talk
to the animals. If you do, they will
talk back to you. But if you
don't talk to the animals,
they won't talk back to you,
then you won't understand, and
when you don't understand you
will fear and when you fear you will
destroy the animals, and if
you destroy the animals,
you will destroy yourself."

- Chief Dan George of the Tsleil-Waututh Nation, author,
poet, and an Academy Award-nominated actor

Chief Dan George, philosopher, poet and Mercado idol.

THE SCRIPPS PROGRAM WAS a life-altering experience for me. For weeks, people kept asking me, "Arthur, how do you keep rebounding against all the odds?" My answer was always the same, "What's the alternative?"

But the real answer was that I was just followed the example of my soul mate, Chief Lone Watie. Who the heck is Chief Lone Watie, you might ask?

My favorite movie of all time is *The Outlaw Josey Wales*. It's a 1976 Revisionist Western movie set at the end of the American Civil War directed by and starring Clint Eastwood (as the eponymous Josey Wales).

An honest-to-goodness Indian chief named Dan George, played the gracious Indian Chief Lone Watie who tried to peacefully coexist with his White brethren. (George, in real life, was head of the Tsleil-Waututh Nation of Indians, located on Burrard Inlet in North Vancouver, British Columbia).

I think I've watched *Josey Wales* at least 50 times. At a particularly poignant moment in the movie, a frustrated

Chief Lone Watie delivers a moving monolog about persevering against the odds. That speech is the story of my life. I have learned I must be strong. I must endure. I must carry on. Every time I watch that scene, I become more committed to endeavor to persevere. Watie said:

> "I'm an Indian all right, but here in The Nations, they call us the civilized tribes. They call us civilized because we are easy to sneak up on. White men have been sneaking up on us for years. They sneaked up on us, and they told us we wouldn't be happy. They told us we would be happy in The Nations. So they took away our tribal lands and sent us here. I had a fine woman and two sons, but they all died on the Trail of Tears.

> "I wore a frock coat to Washington before The War. We wore them because we belonged to the Five Civilized Tribes. We dressed ourselves up like Abraham Lincoln. We got to see the Secretary of the Interior. He said, "Boy, you boys sure look civilized."

> "He congratulated us, and he gave us medals for looking so civilized. We told him about how our tribal lands had been stolen and how our humans were dying. When we finished, he shook our hands and said *"Endeavor to Persevere."*

> "They stood us in a line John Jumper, Chili McIntosh, Buffalo Hump, Jim Buckmark, and me, Lone Watie.

> "Newspapers took our picture and said, "Indians vow to endeavor to persevere." We thought about it for a long time,

endeavor to preserve, and when we had thought about it long enough, we declared war on the Union."

The first time I watched the Chief's speech, chills ran down my spine. I thought about my life, how I never took a shortcut, and always tried to stand up for what was right and decent. Like the Chief, my first line of defense had always been a willingness to compromise, to see the other's point of view. Like the Chief, I only fought when all else failed.

I am certain that my intense desire to persevere has given me the emotional strength to tackle some extraordinary challenges. After ten years by my side, and who knows how many viewings of *Josey Wales*, Susan understands. Completely.

My friend Matt and I had coffee one day after the Healing Heart's Program ended. He paid me the ultimate compliment without knowing it. He said he was taken by my simple philosophy. He mentioned he had studied many of the world's greatest philosophers while obtaining several degrees, but could not place the passages. He asked me for references. I laughed. "It's all in *my* movie." A few days later I lent him my DVD. A week later we shared a cup of coffee and a low-fat muffin at Starbuck's. He handed me a piece of paper. He said, "This is for you." I read the words, a tear formed in my eye. I think it's worth a read.

> As long as I have breath,
> I want for more.
> The less traveled the road,
> The more rewarding my journey.
> Aware destiny rarely changes course,
> I march forward
> against insurmountable odds.
> An inexplicable medical curiosity,
> A phenomenon of a different galaxy.

My pride remains untarnished,
My resolve greater than before,
My dignity in full bloom.
No matter what comes my way,
I shall endeavor to persevere.

© *M.G.Crisci*

~

Endeavoring to persevere has also taught me a few other things on my journey. I call them "bonus insights."

1. *Having good memories is the next best thing to doing what you want to do but can't.*
2. *It's perfectly normal to want to do more with your life, but it's depressing, abnormal to obsess about what you haven't achieved.*
3. *The purpose of life is to avoid being lonely.*

Chapter 52

Lucky #46

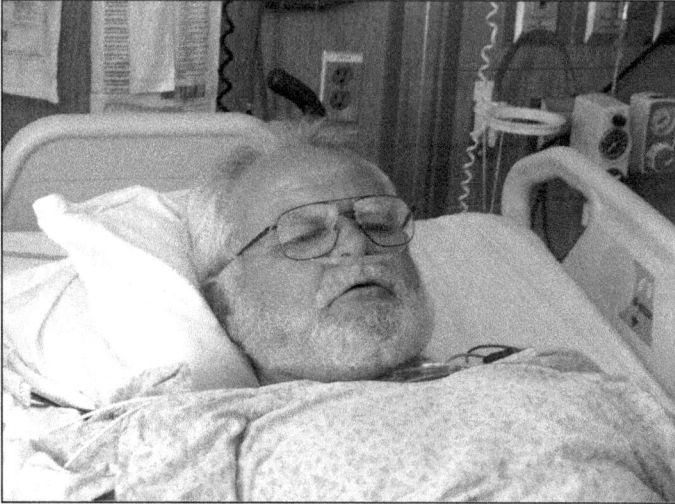

Me resting comfortably minutes after procedure #46.
Crazy Matt says I agreed to take this picture.

I'M FEELING DAMN GOOD!

I've made three new friends in Keith, Kris, and Matt and learned to get my stress more under control.

There was just this one little thing: The angina attacks returned with greater frequency. I was frustrated and confused since I had an angiogram, an angioplasty, a few more stents just months before.

It was also getting harder to sleep through the night without taking a couple of nitro pills for my angina. Two nights ago was the worst. I had to take four nitro pills during the day and another three during the evening. I was surprised to hear the birds chirping at 6:30 a.m. when I opened my eyes. Simply walking was now a chore. I was out of breath after just a few steps.

I visited Dr. Tierstein. Again. I knew what he was going to say before he said it. It was time for another exploratory angiogram. I was certain I'd need at least one stent. I was hoping that was about it. My stent was now 15 (coated and uncoated).

He asked me how bad was my shortness of breath. I lied. I said it was bearable; I didn't want to worry Susan more than she already was. He scheduled the procedure for the following Tuesday, *six days* hence.

I left with a joke. "Doc, I think I'm going to need a second spreadsheet to keep track of all these procedures." (The scheduled procedure was number 46).

On the way home, I began to feel sorry for myself. For the first time, I asked God, "why should one person have to deal with so much stuff? I mean don't I ever get a break?"

God responded warmly. *"Arthur, God may give you little tests. But they are never more than you can handle."*

~

Tuesday took forever to arrive.

The damnedest thing happened along the way. My three new best friends—Keith, Kris, and Matt—visited, called, emailed, and hovered. I could feel the love. I also sensed Susan was impressed and depressed. She realized the situation might be even more serious than usual despite my penchant for joking about matters.

I arrived at the hospital on time. It was 5:30 a.m. (For some reason, heart surgeons love early morning procedures.) Doctor Tierstein stopped by. I was worried. Suppose I needed a stent where another stent had been inserted within another stent?

"Unlikely," he responded.

"Just suppose," I asked. "Will the hardware hold?"

"Arthur, we'll just have to wait and see what we find."

That was not the answer I wanted.

~

About 8:30 a.m. I'm prepped and ready to go. On the way into surgery, I thought about cracking a joke to lighten things up. I resisted the temptation; the last thing I needed was an unsteady hand tried to insert one of those tiny, little suckers into my artery.

As my gurney entered the Cath Lab for the umpteenth time, I couldn't help but notice the new equipment, more modern décor, and brighter lights. The whole nine yards. I wondered if they were testing out new stuff to make sure it worked on patients with better odds?

Next thing I know I'm in that familiar state of Cath Lab twilight. The procedure seemed to send the right signals. The staff was professional but light-hearted, the surgery didn't hurt like the last time, and "the complications team" behind the window stayed behind the window. I even imagined my old buddy, Chief Lone Watie, smiling through the window.

They moved me back to my ICU bay. Time passed. Perhaps 60 minutes. The nurse was smiling as she handed me juice and Jell-O. She was a knock-out. (I always seem to get the cute nurses). She smiled, "Everything went well."

A few minutes later, a beaming Susan appeared. I knew things were okay. She was followed by my friend Matt and his wife, a former nurse, Mary Ann, and my other buddy Kris. I wondered if this is a celebration or a funeral prelude.

"Arthur," Susan said sweetly. "Everything is going to be all right. The doctor told me there was nothing wrong with the prior stent insertions. You just had another spot that needed a little help."

Matt walked over to my bedside and started to make like a doctor analyzing the monitor readouts. He told me my blood pressure was normal, heart rate strong and regular, and my oxygen level was excellent.

I looked at Mary Ann. "Does this yahoo know what the hell he is talking about? She smiled, "Believe it or not, he got it right."

I was so relaxed I decided to take the tiny oxygen tube out of my nose. I mumbled something like "I hate these things. I don't need it." The tube was now sitting on top of me.

Matt was not happy. "Put the f…ing thing back in your nose, you idiot! Do your macho routine some other time. I expect to know you another 20 or 25 years."

Everybody gasped. He was dead serious. I shoved the thing back in. "There, you happy?"

He smiled then pulled out this camera with a huge lens and pointed it at my face. "Okay."

I shook my head. "Okay."

Click, click, click. The nurse returned. "Mr. Mercado, hopefully your photo session is almost done. Lunch will be here any minute." I smiled. "Thank goodness. I'm starved."

"Does lunch include apple pie? Dr. Tierstein said I could have a big piece of apple pie."

I chuckled. My bizarre sense of humor was back.

On cue, Dr. Tierstein appeared. "I don't know about the apple pie, but I think you're a lot of good years left. Plus, there are some new exciting non-invasive protocols to enhance stent performance and durability."

"Like what?" I asked.

"In about six weeks, we're going to *try* some, Enhanced External Counter Pulsation treatments. We'll keep close track of your behavioral responses."

Boy, I thought to myself, that sounds better than a piece of strawberry shortcake smothered in whipped cream!

"Sounds like we're going to be see a lot of each other."

He smiled, "Guess that's one way to put it."

"So, what about I call you Paul?"

Paul laughed. "Arthur, sounds good to me."

Chapter 53

New Best Friend

Renowned cardiologist, Dr. Paul Tierstein (left), his team,
and their Cath Lab buddy, Mother Theresa.

"WHY DON'T WE wait a little longer the next time," said Paul, sarcastically as my gurney was being wheeled *out* of the Cath Lab after yet another procedure.

My first thought, I guess the Enhanced External Pulsation treatments didn't work as expected. I was still woozy, but I could still sense he was more than a bit upset. He mumbled something about not waiting until I was 99% occluded (that's medical double talk for a completely blocked artery). Out of the corner of my eye, I saw Paul (we were now on a first name basis) motion to Susan to meet him in the consult area.

Susan nodded, unaware my friend Matt, who had arrived a little late for the stent party, was standing behind her.

Paul provided comfort *in Paul's way*. "Susan, I believe we can keep Arthur's arteries flowing properly for quite a while, maybe another 40 or so procedures, but he has to be more realistic. When he feels a pain in his chest or arm, he's got to get in here. He can't wait to see if the pain will subside. The artery stent near his lower aorta was 96 per cent blocked when I put him on the table. In my professional opinion, macho man cut it a little close!"

A few hours later, Paul paid a visit to my room and repeated what he had told Susan and Matt. Got me to thinking: *you don't win any prizes for saving a doctor's time by waiting until you are absolutely, positively certain you are dying before you ask for help.*

I decided maybe it was time to accept the obvious: my heart had an expiration date. If Paul performed 40 more cardiovascular procedure every six months, that meant I had about 20 years to live. Put another way, my life warranty "was projected" to expire around age 87, assuming no other complications.

I also realized diet modifications and regular exercise might extend the time between interventions, but they probably wouldn't dramatically alter my final check out date.

Paul wasn't finished. "Arthur, there is some good news in all of this. With the advances in stent technology and what we've been learning about interventions, we should be able to reduce groin interventions." (For those of you who are not familiar with the whole process, the groin is where most stents used to be inserted. Despite what they say, the procedure can be a bit painful, and there is generally some soreness afterward for 4 to 14 days depending upon a lot of factors I'm not about to get into.

Paul continued to wax on. "Moving forward, I anticipate we should be able to enter through the thick fleshy region of your palm near the wrist, and perhaps even some other areas. Obviously, it's a bit early to be too optimistic."

I had two thoughts: How could Paul label any of this optimistic? Secondly, I wished the guy who said in his Amazon 99% of my stories "had to be made up" was on the gurney, instead of me!

~

During the next few weeks, I thought a lot about what Paul. I decided to create a personal balance sheet: you know, the positives and negatives of my projected life warranty.

ON THE POSITIVE SIDE:
- ✓ At age 87 I would have outlived my brother James by 57 years, Pops by 46 and Ernestine Lily Mae by 30.
- ✓ Susan and I would celebrate our silver anniversary. I could eat another burrito or two.
- ✓ I'd outlive Murphy, so he'd never have to be an orphan cat with no father.
- ✓ My coins and sports ceramic collections would grow in value.
- ✓ I'll get to see the first Presidential election where each party spends a billion dollars on advertising.
- ✓ I could tell my weird stories to anybody who would listen at least 1,040 times (assuming of course I only restricted myself to one story a week).
- ✓ I could consume about 145,000 prescription meds (obviously assuming no increase over the 23 a day now).
- ✓ Are there any other positives to knowing when you will probably die? The answer is yes., if you think of it as one of those popular Direct TV commercials.

If you know when you are going to die,
you won't get depressed
and need a psychiatrist.
If you don't need a psychiatrist,
You'll save a lot of money.
With the money you save,

you can buy a fast motorcycle.
With a fast motorcycle,
You can accidentally crash into a wall.
And, if you crash into a wall,
You won't be able to waste money
buying things you don't need.

ON THE NEGATIVE SIDE:

✓   I might only live to see a few great-grandchildren.

✓   I probably won't be around for my golden anniversary.

✓   I won't get to see my beloved Cadillac SUV wear out. (I always believed in taking good care of cars. That way they last longer. Come to think of it, I feel the same way about friends.)

✓   I probably won't experience, energy independence, peace in the Middle East and the Republicans and Democrats working together.

Chapter 54

Parker

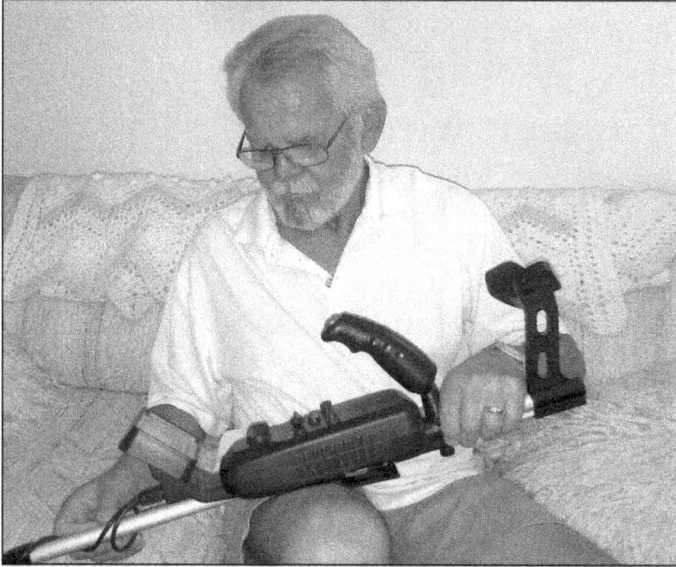

My metal detector is a neat little piece of exercise equipment.

THERE WAS KNOCK ON the door. I glanced at the clock on my night table. It was 2 a.m.

I looked at Susan who was in a deep sleep, figuratively of course. I'm wondering who the hell would come knocking at such an hour. I carefully headed down the stairs, concerned about slipping. (Two weeks earlier, I lost my balance by the fireplace, fell and split my lip. Thanks to the Coumadin, I began to bleed like a sieve. Fortunately, Susan was right there with the gauze pads and bandages.

"Who's there?" I asked. There was no answer. I decided to open the door, even though my gun collection was long since gone! There was nobody anywhere. I waited a few minutes inside my locked front door in case the prankster returned. Nothing. About a half hour later,

I was again awoken from a deep sleep by another knock on the door.

Now, I'm pissed at the prankster. I'm thinking, if only I were younger and stronger, I'd surprise the bastard by running down the back stairs and tackle him from behind. Instead, I peeked out the window from our second-floor bedroom with a cell phone in hand, ready to dial 911. I looked up and down the block. Not a damn thing.

As I closed the window, I couldn't help but notice my hand was still shaking. It finally dawned on me. There was no knock on the door, the sound I heard was my hand banging the headboard as it shook uncontrollably. Being this cool, in control guy, I said nothing to Susan as she left for work later that morning.

A day or so later, Susan and I are getting ready for bed. I'd been on a new medication for Parkinson's that was supposed to reduce the shaking. "Give me a better quality of life," said the specialist. But, as I've learned over the years, there is no such thing as a drug that doesn't have side effects. When I called the doctor's office, the nurse practitioner casually mentioned the drug had been known to cause "some hallucinations in the beginning." Crap, that was the understatement of the year! One dream had my feet separating from my body, and involved some gory stuff streaming out of my head.

One evening it was so bad, I was shaking like a leaf when I woke Susan for comfort. I explained what was happening; she held me tight. I asked her to hold me tighter to make the shaking stop. She did so while whispering gently in my ear, "Arthur, you're not physically shaking. I think it's all in your mind."

And, so it was that I realized my Parkinson's, after almost five years, had begun to move to a new, more unpleasant level.

~

The other day Matt called to invite himself over for a cup of coffee. He asked if I wanted him to pick up anything to eat. I responded "donuts." He laughed. "No problem, do you like jelly donuts?" I responded I love jelly donuts, but these days I get so excited when I try to hold a jelly donut the stuff starts squirting out." *If you've got Parkinson's enjoy any kind of donuts you want, so long as they're not filled with jelly, custard or cream.*

He began to laugh his ass off! Eventually, we settled on three glazed donuts, two cinnamon donuts, and a chocolate covered donut.

Another lesson learned. *Don't ever lose your sense of humor. And, if you don't have any, go find one.*

~

As Parkinson's progresses, even little thing like getting out of a chair becomes just a little bit harder.

The other day was just one of those days: I was struggling to get up from a kitchen chair. There was another chair nearby. I placed my hand on it without applying pressure and was able to get up real easy. I thought to myself, maybe I'm coddling myself a bit too much. So, I tried to get up again without the chair. I slipped then struggled to regain my footing with both chairs.

My conclusion: *If you've got a physical limitation, don't be a jerk. Macho workarounds can be hazardous to your health!*

Parkin's also has an artistic side. Imagine, you've got a box of beautiful crayons. Just take one crayon out at a time, and let your hand shake on a piece of paper. Then add another color and another. When you decide to stop, look at the beautiful color image you've created.

To me, Parkinson's is like an unplanned visit from an unwanted relative. Before you know it, the damn guy moves in permanently. To place a name with the face, I've decided to call my unwanted friend Parker because he has decided to "park" himself in my house!

Between Parker and my patched-up ticker, I don't know if I'll ever get to stage five Parkinson's or whatever they call it is when you need round-the-clock supervision. But, I look at it this way, if my heart wins the race it gets a gold medal for cheating Parker spreading his final mayhem!

~

Susan also decided to invite a friend. He's called exercise.

God bless her, after putting in a full day at the office, she comes home and takes a walk with me. Sometimes a mile, sometimes more. Completing the walk makes me feel more alert physically; it's also improved my mental because I know I've accomplished something positive. (Hope that makes sense. Sometimes, I don't explain things too well).

Recently, I decided to make my own exercise initiative. I searched the garage for my old metal detector. Once in hand, my mind was flooded with recollections.

When I lived in L.A., I'd walk around the beach for miles with my detector in search of stuff that people lost play volleyball, dragging kid's paraphernalia, and putting their umbrellas up and down. In addition to getting exercise and a nice tan, I found coins, jewelry, watches, beer and wine openers, and other cool stuff. During my trial and error period, I learned the best time to metal detect was after a rain storm or a high tide because the sand would shift, and good stuff would get buried inches below the sand line.

I also learned the speed of removal was important. So, when the metal dictator registered dead center, I'd take a four-inch ice pick out of my pocket and jab the ground until the object became visible.

I knew I no longer lived by a beach, but there were plenty of parks where kids and their parents played. I shook my head; Artie wouldn't do stuff like that anymore. Today, if I find anything of value, I go out of my way to find the rightful owner. I sat paralyzed wondering what to do.

A few days, I explained my dilemma to Matt. He said, "Why not bag the ice pick, and just walk around the park with the metal detector; you'll get some exercise and build upper body strength." I nodded, the idea didn't sound half bad. We decided to test it out. He drove me to the park, and I walked around for about 30 minutes while he sat on a nearby park bench.

A police car drove up and stopped. "What the hell are you guys doing?"

Chapter 55

September

*My friend Matt and I were poster children
for the Scripps Integrative Medicine Magazine.*

I KEEP TELLING MYSELF it's been all good as I approach the September of my years.

(September makes me sound smarter than I am and suggests there is a lot of thread left on the tires).

Plus, my unusual sense of humor remains intact; I've got a loving wife, a super-special, independent-minded daughter, four wonderful grandkids, a terrific son-in-law, and a bunch of close friends. Hell, I've even got cardiologist who has convinced me that I'm mortal, and when I feel pain in my shoulder it's probably not just angina, but a blockage that needs a little immediate R&R (repair and recalibration).

I've sorta lost track, but I think we are up to 27 or 28 stents. On one of my recent visits to the Cath Lab, my buddy Matt came along for moral support. He was pleased and surprised they let him into the prep area. I told him I had been there so many times that I was now a *Scripps Cath Lab Platinum Club Member*, which gave me unique group visitation privileges that ordinary patients simply did not qualify for!

He was amazed that everybody seemed to know me. All he could talk about was the cordial, first class treatment I received.

"Mr. Mercado, so nice to see you gain."

"Mr. Mercado, you're looking very well considering."

"Mr. Mercado is there anything we can do to make you more comfortable?"

Matt was amazed at the cordial, personalized service. "Artie," he said (He calls me Artie. Personally, I think it sounds ridiculous to call a 70-year-old man 'Artie'), "the staff treats you like they treat regulars at the Four Seasons Hotel."

"That's why I keep coming back," I responded. "First class service without those ridiculous Four Seasons' prices."

~

Matt said, "Artie, I have an idea."

With him, I've learned that not necessarily a good thing.

"How would you like to be featured in the *Ripley Books of Records?*"

I responded, "What the hell are you talking about?"

"You've got to be close to the record for total stents inserted in one human being."

After some more conversation, he convinced me to pull out all my medical records, so we could how many. The problem was we couldn't find some of my early paper records. The ones before computers.

"Matt's was disappointed but not out of ideas. "Jesus when you all this heart procedures (he meant the stents plus angiograms, angioplasties, endarterectomies, etc.), you've got to hold the world record for *the most heart procedures without actually dying.*"

I asked him if there was such a category. He said if there wasn't one, there should be!

~

During my journey to September, I've also learned few things about so-called routine invasive procedures.

First, there is no such thing. What may be normal for me, might not be for you. And, nobody has any way of predicting in advance.

Here's an example. My friend Don had a torn knee meniscus which required arthroscopic surgery; they shaved the edges and told him he was good as new. Three days later he cycled five miles on his stationery bike.

Don told another mutual friend who was about to undergo essentially the same procedure "it's a piece of cake." Well, the other guy, my buddy Matt. It turned out his tear was larger than originally assumed. After painkillers and three months of physical therapy, he *started* to feel normal.

Second. Remember heart surgery is a lot like gambling. Do everything you can to improve the odds. Try to book a well-respected surgeon; preferably someone experienced with your kind of medical history.

Not a bad idea to make sure you are tended by experienced nurses. That can reduce the usual post procedure angst. Hell, they may even know what kind of fruit juice you like.

Third. Listen to the damn doctor when he says, "Take the time you need to recuperate, before getting physically ambitious. When I was in my younger, more immortal stage, I was determined to playing golf a day or two after a procedure. It seemed important to me to prove something. As I look back now, I have no idea what I was trying to prove.

Four. Try to do something physical. Walk, crawl, grovel, raise your legs, punch a wall, throw beans bags in a garbage pail, open beer bottles. The key is to do something repetitively.

Five. Maintain a proper attitude. Don't sit home and feel sorry for yourself, or wonder why it happened to me. It doesn't matter. It is what it is.

Recently, Matt told me about this Australian singer, Slim Dusty, who made Waltzing Matilda famous. He also wrote a less-known song called, *You've Got to Taste the Foam to Drink the Beer.* The first time I listened, it thought it was corny, even for me. But, the more I played it, the more I realized the lyrics were a self-help guide that could put those expensive psychiatrists out of business.

> *There's some who like to protest and a lot who*
> *like to moan*
> *And no one wants to pay their tax or the interest*
> *on their loan*
> *But as you struggle on through life for all that you*
> *hold dear*
> *Remember that you've gotta drink the froth to get*
> *the beer...*
> *Don't waste your time complainin' cause no one*
> *wants to know*
> *In life there's no rehearsal it's straight on with the*
> *show*
> *As you're roarin' down a highway smooth as a*
> *feather bed*
> *Keep an eye out for a sign that says gravel road*
> *ahead*
> *No matter what you read or no matter what you*
> *hear it's a laydown hand you bet you're gonna*
> *pay for all you get*
> *Hey, you've gotta drink the froth to get the beer.*
> © *Slim Dusty*

Old Slim did miss one point. *In life, some people get more froth in their mug than beer. Don't take it personally; the tap was probably one of those cheap Chinese imports.*

Chapter 56

Call Me Crazy

Nurse Sherrie convinced me to participate.
Most of my friends thought I had finally lost it.

PARTICIPATING IN A FIVE-MILE Walk-a-Thon was never part of my life plan, even though I *accidentally* began preparing for it 12 months ago.

I sat in front of my cardiologist, Paul, who gave me the all-too-familiar diagnosis: "Arthur, your latest X-Rays indicate that one of so and so artery is 98 percent blocked." I thought to myself, here we go again, another trip to the Cath Lab is just days away. But Paul had a surprising revelation.

"Unfortunately, Arthur, certain arteries can only hold so many stents. That one has a stent within a stent. So, our usual solution may not be available. We'll just have to see."

I thought to myself, see about what? How long does it take to die when you are 100% clogged? I began to laugh. "Paul, are you sure we can't pop a few more in there?"

Paul nodded sadly.

I responded cheerfully. "I don't think it's quite time yet. No worries Doc; I'll figure out a workaround. Over the last 30 years, I've become creative at workarounds, particularly when somebody says there ain't no more. *Gotta remember, Doctors are human, they can only do so much, after that it up to you to keep it going.*

That having been said, I long ago promised myself when it was time; I'd go quietly with my dignity intact. The last thing I want is people standing over my grave talking about how bad I looked at the end. And, I don't want things to drag out, causing pain for those I love. I just want to pick up my suitcase at the front door and head out. No muss, no fuss, no stress.

My intuition or determination or both told me it wasn't time yet, despite the 98 percent blockage. The way I look at it, if somebody says you can't do something 98 percent of the time that means *you can do something* at least *twice* more!

There and then, I decided to make one of *my twices* the most aggressive walking program I could. The walk had to take place in pleasant non-athletic surroundings, with no crowds or unnecessary complications like driving my car somewhere and then figuring out how to park it. It turned out there was a perfect one-mile stretch that began and ended right at my front door: a couple of turns, two reasonably decent hills, and flat cool down section.

~

My original goal was to see how far I could go a few days a week. I started by doing about a third-of-a-mile before I lost my breath. A month later I was doing half-a-mile. Three months later, I walked the entire course for the first time. As tired as I was, I felt like Rocky on the museum steps in Philadelphia.

Another visit to my cardiologist confirmed my exercise routine was "all good." My 98% blockage was still only 98%! I decided it would be nice to have a walking buddy, so I convinced Susan to join me...after she put in a full day's work at the office. Told her it would be good for the both of us. She readily agreed. She's a great partner, my best friend, and a hell of a good sport. At first, we did my little course three days a week, then four. Now we walk our course every day of the week around 5:30 PM! Along the way, we see many of our neighbors doing their little chores and cheering us on. That is a great morale booster.

In some ways, the hour together has made us even closer. We *talk about the little things in life that may not seem important but mean everything when two people love each other.* As I mentioned earlier, my Parkinson's is moving along nicely. I notice I tend to lose thoughts more frequently. I guess *one of the best things about Parkinson's is the further it progresses the less you remember that you forgot something.*

Not too long ago, I was discussing my walking routine with my fun-loving Parkinson's nurse practitioner from Scripps, Sherrie Gould. She said she was proud of me fighting the good fight. She leaned back in her chair and paused for a moment.

"Arthur, I have an idea."

I don't like surprises, never have. But, I felt one coming.

"Ever heard of the San Diego Walk-a-Thon."

"Nope."

"It's an annual event where people walk five kilometers to raise awareness of Parkinson's among the general public. Why not sign-up?"

My first reaction...Five kilometers, you've got to be kidding! My second thought was, what the hell, why not? Worst case it will kill me.

Susan was with Sherrie (women always stick together) sensed my skepticism. "Arthur, think of the walk-a-thon as a free workout under a doctors' supervision," she said sweetly. "Besides, it's such a good cause. I thought you wanted people to know more about living with Parkinson's, so they wouldn't be afraid."

It was two against one of me. How could I say no?

~

Three Saturdays later, I checked into the starter area with a thousand or so participants, some screaming kids, chatty, well-meaning parents, and loud hip-hop music.

As I walked to the starter line, I got quite anxious. I had second thoughts. What the hell am I doing here? Do I really want to do this?

Suddenly, a gun sounded and I just start walking. At that point, I wasn't thinking about winning or even finishing; I just wondered how far I could go. I took comfort in the fact that Susan was by my side watching every step, every breath. The further we walked, the more people dropped like flies. To my surprise, I didn't start to get tired till the two-kilometer mark (about 1 ½ miles, or 50% more than I'd ever walked). Susan smiled and asked if I wanted to stop. I shook my head, "hell no." I thought to myself; we might as well find out how far this stubborn, Cath-Lab worn body can still travel.

In truth, I felt some aches and pains I hadn't experienced in quite a while. But, with each step, I became more confident I could take another. Twenty-seven minutes later we passed the four-kilometer marker. I could see the finish line in the distance. I could also see one last steep incline. It was like a footbridge on steroids. Suddenly I remembered I had a fear of heights— elevators, escalators, even six-foot ladders.

I recalled my father sticking me on a picket fence when I was three years old. He was telling me it was okay to be afraid, but just don't let the fear stop you from doing what you want to do.

I paused. Pop would have been proud! Despite my initial case of the shakes, I had done exactly what I set out to do. I walked 4.5 kilometers, which topped my personal best by 45 per cent.

Chapter 57

Top Eight

Life is like a labyrinth. You don't know how you got there,
and you're not sure how to get out.

THESE DAYS IT SEEMS everybody is worried about hurting somebody's feelings, so people rarely express how they feel.

But I must admit, in my case, it works a little different. When people hear the story about all my heart stuff, they look at me, and say they can't believe it, "You look so happy and healthy."

My usual response? Crack a joke. Something like, "Looking good because I'm a man with no worries. The last time I spoke to God, he told me to enjoy myself, said he'd give me plenty of notice when it was time."

Sometimes they laugh, sometimes they feel awkward and look toward the floor or the front door. The important thing is that I crack myself up.

Another thing that seems to happen more often these days when people visit—my hand starts slapping the side of my leg. They notice but are usually tongue-twisted. That's when I say, "Oh, did I forget to mention, I've got a little Parkinson's. My cardiologist tells me the shaking activity is a good exercise for my heart." That usually makes the awkwardness disappear.

Having Parkinson's is no picnic, and I'm well aware it's not going to miraculously get better. But, I'm be damned if going to walk around moaning woe is me. In fact, as I deal with the challenges of the disease, I've discovered there are a lot of reasons to love Parkinson's. Check this out!

PAPA CADO'S TOP EIGHT LIST

1. *Parkinson's helps you eat more of what you like without gaining weight.*

I love eating. It's one of the great pleasures in life. Recently, I noticed the Parkinson's was now causing me to see double a lot of the time. I also noticed, when I ate I had twice as much food in front of me. Conclusion? I can now eat twice as much of the stuff I like, and not put on any additional weight.

2. *You never have to do things you don't want to do.*

I always make it a point to make sure people know I have Parkinson's. *Sometimes*, they get overly dramatic which I'm not crazy about. But, they *always* give me lots of slack because they always assume I forget most things. So, when my friends or family suggest I really should do this or that, because it's good for me, and I don't agree, I don't argue or debate. I just don't do it. When they ask why I didn't take their suggestion, I just say I forgot. Works every time!

3. *Parkinson's eliminates idle phone chatter with boring people*

Imagine somebody calls. You've said all you want to say, but the other person wants to keep yakking. I've never been a confrontational person, so I find it hard to say, "Let's hang up." What I do is let my Parkinson's do the talking. I take my shaking hand and tap near the phone so that the caller can hear it. Inevitably, the person says, "Arthur, what's that noise?" I say, "Oh, that's just my Parkinson's acting up."

4.   *Parkinson's eliminates worthless text message clutter.*

I think young people today find talking to each other too much work. They'd rather spend the time sending text messages and email, half of which require another text or email to explain what they meant to say. These days you can't even stand in line at McDonald's without noticing people pressing little buttons. That's why having Parkinson's can be a blessing.

My hand isn't steady enough to tap all those little keys without having to redo and redo. By then I've usually forgotten what I was texting about. I've still got one of those flip phones with the big numbers and buttons. That way I can pick up the phone when somebody calls, or if I've got a medical emergency, I can get help right away. My response to those who say I sound like an old fuddy-duddy, you're right, and I'm proud of it!

5.   *Parkinson's helps lower my blood pressure.*

Because I forget a lot of stuff so quickly now, I never worry much about who I was supposed to call, or what I was supposed to do. I figure if it's all that important they'll make the extra effort to get a hold of me or remind me of what I'm supposed to do. For example, if I'm scheduled to take a medication or go to the doctor, I know Susan's there to remind me. And, if I'm going out to lunch with a friend, and I forget, they'll give me all the time I need to get ready. Having so much slack makes life stress-free, tends to lower my blood pressure. Susan would argue it's the medications. I just let her think that! Like I said, stress-free!

6.   *Parkinson's can sharpen your mental A-CU-I-TY.*

Gotta admit, a-cu-i-ty is not part of my standard vocabulary. But I've developed the little home-made Mercado process to help that acuity thing.

When I start shaking, my goals are always the same: first, slow it down; then to make it stop altogether.

To slow thinsg down, I grab the shaking hand with my other hand and hold it for 30-60 seconds. Then, I grab my leg, which may or may not be shaking, it doesn't matter, and hold it for another 30-60 seconds with my good hand.

While I'm running through my physical routine, I force my mind to concentrate on one thing, and only one thing…coming to a screeching halt. Believe it or not, most of the damn time it works. My suggestion? *Give yourself credit, your mind is a lot stronger than you think.*

7.   *Parkinson's improves your physical appearance.*

In my case, I've been self-conscious about my appearance for almost 40 years.

You see I had this buddy, Rudy, who worked for me 40 years ago when I was the quality control manager in Glendale, California. He was crazy about this cute little blonde secretary and wanted to ask her out. Rudy figured it would be easier for her to say yes if it was a double date. He convinced the blonde (sorry can't remember her name) to ask her girlfriend to join us.

I heard the girls talking it over on the other side of a partition. The double date prospect (can't remember her name either) tells her friend, "no way, that guy Arthur looks like a frog."

So, from that day on, I grew a mustache and beard, which I maintain to this day. The funny thing is, when I go to a barber shop now, and, people hear I have Parkinson's they always say the same thing, "Man, you look great, would have never guessed."

8.   *Parkinson's makes you sound smarter than you are.*

I'm one of those people who always tells things as they are. And, while I don't intentionally go out of my way to insult people, but I have been known to ruffle a few feathers.

These days I notice I start sentences then forget what I want to say next. So, I've taught myself to pause, and think harder. People notice the pause, whether in person or on the phone. But, they never say anything. They just wait patiently. Damndest thing, when I finally cobble something together, it's generally logical. In fact, they seem to think I'm smarter than I am because I pause so much before I speak.

Chapter 58

Nightmares

Drug interactions can sure stimulate the old creative juices.

THIS IS A TOUGH CHAPTER for me to write. But I think anyone who travels into the invisible darkness of Parkinson's can use a little light to show them the way.

Let's start with the good news first. The pharmaceutical manufacturers have come up with lots of drugs to slow your trip.

And, the Madison Avenue guys and girls have generated fancy names like Sinemet, Symmetrel, Eldepryl and Tasmar that will make you feel like you're about to receive manna from heaven.

But here's the deal, none of them will allow you to change the end game. *Parkinson's is like a baseball player labeled good-field, no-hit. He may have a season or two where he exceeds expectations, but eventually, his weak bat brings him back to reality.*

~

I mention that because the doctors have worked like hell to give me more quality time. But, it has come at a cost. As we've mixed and matched meds, changed doses, etc., there has been a dramatic increase in nightmares. I'm told that simply "a common side effect." Now isn't that great?

Like every unexpected twist and turn on my journey, I've just learned to deal with it. In fact, I have two *recurring nightmares that could make great videos on YouTube!*

One nightmare involves me searching for the daughter I abandoned at birth. I'm walking through this forest of scary monsters that are very hard to describe. All I remember is they're mad as hell. Out of nowhere appears this little girl. She's in front of me with her back turned. I never actually see her face. Just some long brown curls. She calls out, "Dad, Dad." I run toward her. But every time I think I'm getting close, I come to this deep ravine, and stop at the edge to prevent falling into the darkness. I cry out to her, but to no avail.

In the second nightmare, there is some guy with a deep voice who keeps telling me to stand still. When I do, he starts ripping off my arms and legs. It gets pretty gory. My shirt is rather stained to say the least. The scene is so frightening that I wake up to find my hand is tapping the headboard. The ruckus almost always wakes up Susan who just keeps her cool and holds my hand until I calm down. The best way to describe what I see is to imagine of one those tortured artists who paint weird images that wind up in museums where critics call the stuff "insightful and tortured."

I know I've had many other nightmares, but I only remember weird bits and pieces. The do one thing they have in common, they all scare the crap out of me, and they don't go away.

The other thing I've noticed is that the higher we make my meds doses to control the shaking during the day, the more nightmares I have at night.

But the way I look at it, that's not all bad. The short scary nights give me long days to experience the magnificent Southern California sunshine, talk to my friends, sit on our colorful little patio to think about what a great life I've had.

People like happy people. Even sad people. So if you want friends to stick around, don't start making jokes about your weird, depressing nightmares.

~

I also like to take the occasional short walk without a walker. Sometimes I tell Susan, and sometimes I don't for fear of her calling the neighbors to watch me from their windows. Like everything in life, my walks are both good and bad news. My determination to walk without a walker brings me the satisfaction of achieving something. The bad news is that this same sense of determination has caused a few dropsies, a few bruises and a few cuts that required medical assistance.

In closing, a few words of wisdom.

Drug-induced nightmares are a lot like being married to the wrong women. Just learn to make the best of a bad situation.

Chapter 59

Back & Forth

Celebrating New Year's Eve with Susan and the swordfish.

BY MY STANDARDS, I'VE had a good run during the last nine months. Yes, I've had a few more stents, and the Parkinson's has gotten a little worse, but I'm happy to report, I'm fighting the good fight. My spirits are good; the latest stents seem to be doing their job; my return to exercise has sharpened my faculties and boosted self-confidence.

Arthur: Based on Paul's projections I am somewhere between the October and December of my life here. And, that's all good.

Susan: My main job these days, in addition to my regular job, is to keep Arthur active. It is amazing what a little exercise will do for the body and the mind. I know he also likes to chat with friends like Wally the fish, Buddy the dog (now departed) and Murphy, the cat, although I do wonder what could they possibly have in common?

I also don't agree with Arthur's estimate that he is somewhere between October and December. With his sense of humor and fierce determination, he'll probably outlive us all.

Arthur: As you can imagine, I'm finally learned to treat my health issues a bit more realistically. But, Susan and my friends tell me my "unusual sense of humor" still seems to be intact. I mean, if you can't laugh at the hand you've been dealt, how would you get through every day?

Susan: Another case of agree-disagree. He "says" he treats his health more realistically, then I find out he's slipped out to lunch with Matt and comes home raving about a chorizo burrito at the local Mexican restaurant. The man also loves his sweets. He'll pass up a tasty, fresh salad with Balsamic vinegar for a piece of peach pie a la mode every day of the week. But, I do agree, he has an extraordinary sense of humor. He made me laugh the first time we met, and he still does.

Arthur: I'm also being extra careful about the bees near our house because we've discovered I'm grossly allergic to them. And, getting in and out of the car requires a bit more care and attention than it used to. But, most people say I look great, and those that meet me for the first time, can't believe my little journey through life.

Susan: He's not kidding about those aggressive bees. Ask the fellow who lives down the street from us. And, somewhat vainly I would say, we both look pretty good despite all the bumps in the road.

Arthur: Bees or no bees, Parkinson's or no Parkinson's, a weak heart or no weak heart, I still love to eat. So, this New Year's Eve I suggested to Susan we have a nice steak dinner with a few friends. Worst case, is I wind up with a little indigestion.

Susan: Agreed. Good for the old man to get out with friends. Not sure New Year's Eve was the best time, but he insisted. We struck a deal. I said yes to New Year's Eve, but no to steak. Too much fat. P.S. He loved the swordfish!

~

Arthur: Well as you can see from the back and forth I'm in good hands. Susan has been an amazing partner on my rather unusual journey. *So, to all those people who get irritated at one time or another by a spouse, loved one, or partner, get over it, the grass is not greener on the other side. It just a muddy field of weeds.*

On a purely personal note, I am proud and honored that you've gotten this far in the book. I hope it makes your day just a little better.

Susan: Me too!

Arthur: You won't believe this, but there is more.

Susan: Quite a bit more, and so Arthur!

Chapter 60

50 Years Later

My life remains one never-ending surprise after another.

NOT LONG AGO SUSAN retired from her position at a local pharmaceutical company. When she worked, we'd talk two or three times a day on my flip phone. Nothing big, just a quick check-in to make sure I was safe and sound. Why a flip phone? Think about it... those tiny smartphone keys aren't so smart for people with Parkinson's. Besides, *if a flip phone is good enough for Warren Buffet, it's good enough for me.*

Boy has life changed! Now Susan watches my every move, twenty-four seven. She is my exercise buddy, my social director, and my caregiver. She cheers me up when I'm, feeling a little bit down and holds my hand gently when I can't quite remember what I want to say.

A few months back, she retrieved the mail, walked into the living room and handed me a hand-written envelope with an unfamiliar return address: Teresa

Engilman, Sacramento, California. The writer explained she was born 50 years ago, in Baldwin Park, California, and had been adopted by a "Daniel and Anne Engilman who had provided her a decent life and been decent parents."

Teresa said she didn't want to create any disruption or pain; "I just want to express my gratitude to my biological father and mother for the selfless act of making sure I was part of a good family." She mentioned she had found her mother, a woman named Diane Foreman Harris, who gave her my name.

I showed the letter to Susan who knew all about my relationship with Diane and the baby we gave up for adoption.

Susan read it and nodded. She knew that this was an important but incomplete chapter of my life.

We both agreed the letter was real, and Susan helped me respond. I explained:

I was her father and so happy to get her letter.

I told her about her half-sister Mindy and her four step-nieces, my granddaughters, Savannah, Summer, Sierra, and Serena.

I also explained I had some major heart issues and was battling Parkinson's. "I'm pretty tough and hanging in there,"

I told I'd had an interesting life, and that much of it was chronicled in a book called *Papa Cado* written by a dear friend.

I told her I'd like to meet her if she could find her way to San Diego. And, maybe give me bring some pictures, so I could get to know my long, lost daughter.

I didn't ask what ever happened to her mother, Diane, but I was curious, to say the least.

When we finished writing, I asked Susan if she thought the letter was too sappy. *If you want to complain about the hand you've been dealt, play solitaire. That way nobody has to listen to you moan and groan.*

Susan responded, "absolutely not."

~

About nine days later, an email arrives. Teresa explained she had read the book about my life. "Dad, now I know where my quick wit and humor come from. I was born a smart ass and haven't changed."

She then said something that made me smile and cry at the same time. *"I've learned that wit and humor are necessary to get through life's tougher moments. It's a lot better than crawling into a corner and letting the world beat the crap out of you."*

I shook my head with pride. "Couldn't have said it better myself." Susan agreed. Teresa had a healthy dose of my genes.

Her letter continued. "Another thing I've learned is that you have to unconditional love for those who love you. I want you to know I have never felt so happy having you, my mom, and Susan in my life. I want it to last forever. Sorry, you're stuck with me now. I hope that's okay.

She explained she would be coming down to spend time with me on September 20th.

~

Shortly after I received Teresa second letter, I had another setback. I was again hospitalized. It was a strange situation. I knew I was losing my thoughts more frequently, but at the same time, I wanted to hold out to me my daughter. I counted the days till the 20th.

Susan met Teresa at the door to my room. All I could see was her back and her long brown curls, like the girl in my nightmare. Susan smiled, "Arthur, say hello to your daughter Teresa." She smiled, then hugged me. I cried. She cried. Susan cried.

Teresa had brought a picture book of her life to date. Her face was filled with that mischievous Mercado twinkle. "Dad, I thought you might want to see what you've missed these last 50 years."

The whole thing was a bit overwhelming given my foggy state. I tried to process the pictures of all the people in Teresa's life as she slowly turned the pages at my bedside. I know I stared and stared. Then, I did my best impersonation of a dumb father. "Now that was cool," I said.

Teresa smiled, then got up and walked to the door, "some else would like to say hello." There stood Diane...

Chapter 61

Final Rest

My favorite hobby: Collecting vintage baseball cards.

At 9:07 PM, Pacific Coast Time, on Friday, September 30, 2016, Arthur La Voughn Mercado, 72, aka Papa Cado, traveled to his final rest. There, he was joined his mother Lilia Mae, father Big Art, and brother James aka Ernie.

He passed peacefully, without pain, and, in a manner that placed an exclamation point on his extraordinary journey through life.

Arthur is survived by his wife Susan, two daughters, Mindy and Teresa, four grandchildren, Savannah, Summer, Sierra and Serena, high school sweetheart, Diane, Murphy the cat, and his fabulous collection of vintage baseball cards.

> You shall cross the barren desert,
> but you shall not die of thirst.
> You shall wander far in safety
> though you do not know the way.
> You shall speak your words in foreign
> lands , and all will understand.
> You shall see the face of God and live.

Be not afraid.
I go before you always.
Come follow me, and
I will give you rest.

If you pass through raging waters in the sea,
you shall not drown.
If you walk amid the burning flames,
you shall not be harmed.
If you stand before the power of hell
and death is at your side, know that
I am with you through it all.

Be not afraid.
I go before you always.
Come follow me, and
I will give you rest.

© Bob Dufford, S.J.

Part Five

Letters from Arthur

✔ To Pop

Dear Pop,

It's been almost 40 years since we've communicated directly. It's cliché, but I think of you often.

While certain memories have begun to blur at the edges, others remain crystal clear. I remember the day you died like it was yesterday. You were a tower of strength, my tower of strength. I thought you were invincible. When they told me you died pushing an off-road bike up a hill, I smiled. My first thought was how could a hill ever beat my Pop?

Thankfully in our short time together, you left me value systems, endless situational roadmaps, and very clear directions.

I just wanted to let you know that your youngest son did okay. I never became the richest guy in the world, and God knows I'm not exactly Brad Pitt. (You probably don't know who that is. He was voted the world's sexiest man a few years back!) But I have tried to do as you showed me. I always put in an honest day's work. Nobody can ever say Big Art's son was a slacker.

I always tried to tell it like it was. Although sometimes, it might have been better if I sugar coated the truth. You know most people are not built for straight ahead. And when I could, I gave more than I could. But compared to your amazing generosity, I have been a pauper.

I'm also proud to report your youngest has laughed his way through his first 65 years. Although between the mistakes in judgment, the excesses, and the health-related setbacks, there have been times when I could have cried. During those darkest moments, I said to myself, what would Pop have done in this situation? Then I kicked myself in the butt and got up off the canvas. Recently, I added Parkinson's disease to my list of ailments, so I have this shake. I was self-conscious at first, now I just laugh. One day, this attractive nurse is taking my blood pressure. She didn't know about my condition. She thought I was nervous about the reading. I said, "Naaah, I just get shook up around pretty women." She laughed. I stopped shaking, and that was that.

How are Mom and James? You guys left Lori and me hanging. (That was supposed to be a joke!). In any event, I do have some important news. I hope it isn't redundant since I'm not sure what you hear about up there. Simply put, your son's health is failing big time. There is still so much I'd like to do for Susan, Mindy and the grandkids. But I'm tired. Remember the repairs we made on that 1928 Ford? Well, multiply those by ten, and that will give you an idea of the patches and plugs the doctors have applied to this weary body.

I have this feeling we'll be talking face-to-face real soon. Then again, maybe I'll keep beating the odds. The doctors no longer call me Arthur. They call me "tough guy." Remember when you named me that?

With Love and Pride,
Little Art

✓ To Mom

Dear Mom,

The other day I was watching John Wayne in the movie, *True Grit*. It's become one of my all-times favorites. It so much reminds me of your fierce determination, your inner strength.

People used to assume I got my grit from big Art, but you and I both know, I had more of Ernestine's genes than Art's.

At first, I wondered why, with Lori and James both being older than me, you came to rely on me so much. As time went on, I realized why, and I was honored to be your "go-to son." Although, I should tell you, from time to time I wondered what the hell was running through your mind. I remember you naming those crazy dogs Pitzi and Chi-Chi. Pitzi, I could live with Pitzi, but, for goodness sake, Chi-Chi meant tits in Spanish. What was that all about?

Then there was that mobile park you wanted to live in after Pop passed. Remember that patch of gravel in the back? I still remember the call. "Arthur, I want to change the back yard from gravel to real grass. It will brighten my day. Would you do that for me?" You knew the answer. So, there I was digging up the gravel and dragging it down the road to my truck, tilling the soil, installing sprinklers and sod. I can still remember the sweat pouring off me in the heat, but the look on your face when I finished made it all worthwhile. I still have the question you never answered. Why did you make me come back three months later and replace the grass with gravel? Was that supposed to be a personal toughness test? Or was that just you being Mom? I never said much at the time. Because Pop taught me, what Mom wants, Mom gets.

I also wanted to let you know; I'm so sorry you suffered so much during your lifetime. I never understood why God selected such a little lady to carry such a big burden. But you never whined or complained. That's another legacy you gave me.

You know, my only regret is that night at the hospital. I still believe if I had been there, you'd still be here.

Gotta go now. Getting ready for my thirty-something heart procedure. See you soon.

Love from your favorite son,
Arthur

✓ To Ernie

Dear Ernie,

James, do you have any idea why Lori and I started calling you Ernie? Neither of us can remember. If you recall, let us know. But that's not the reason I'm writing today. I just wanted to let you know I still miss all the good times we had as kids, as teenagers, and as grown-ups (although I'm not sure we ever made it to real grown-ups).

The other day, I was sitting in traffic waiting for the light to change, and this vintage red Ford Mustang 390 pulls up next to me. Remember? There we were, brother and brother driving those new hot cars, you in your Mustang and me in my Triumph GT6. Weren't we the coolest things in that bar that night? I thought it was hysterical the way you flipped out when we went to the parking lot, and you found the guy in the next space had scraped the hell out of your car door. I guess I would have had a similar "Mercado reaction" if that was me. But you standing on the hood of that guy's car at 2 a.m. stomping on his hood is an image I'll never forget.

When you left here so suddenly, I cried privately for a long time. You were my forever pal. I assume you are aware that when you died, we had you cremated. I carried your jar next to me in the car to the cemetery. It was the longest trip I ever made in my car.

I'm guessing you've heard I've had a few rough spots of my own. But like Mom used to say, I'm still kicking and ticking. In fact, compared to most, I've had a great life.

I was wondering if it would be all right to give you a call occasionally? The older I get, the more I miss you. Please email your latest phone number when you get this letter.

See you soon,
Bro

✔ To Lori

Dear Sis,

I'm not sure I've ever flat out said it this way, but I wanted you to know I've always been proud that you're my big sister. I think about you and, yes, worry about you all the time.

My mind is filled with memories of a beautiful young lady. So much fun. So full of life. Remember your photo portfolio? The movie star dreams? I still have that picture of you caressing that tree. As they say today, you were a hot babe.

I almost had neighborhood bragging rights when you came so close to modeling for that magazine. That seems like a million years and a million tears ago.

Relationships always seem to have dealt you a tough hand, and that makes me feel bad. I always wished I could have found and introduced you to the man of your dreams. Crazy as it might sound, your baby brother found the love of his life late in life, so keep swinging, there's time yet.

When I think back over my life to date, I have but one real regret...that I could not have done more for you. I'm not sure I know what that means exactly, but we are the last Mercado's standing, so maybe enlightenment will shine my way.

Just remember, as long as I'm here, I'm always there for you.

Your loving baby brother,
Arthur

✔ To Mindy

Dear Mindy Phoo,

What does the proudest father in the world say to the best daughter in the world? As you know, I was never too good with words, although I was always comfortable telling you know how much I loved you.

I guess in our day, we were trail blazers. I mean, how many Pops got to raise their daughters by themselves? In addition to love, I always tried to give you values, perspective, and a little of Pop and Grandma Ernestine's determination, grit, self-reliance, and generosity.

When I talk to you on the phone, see Jimmy and the kids, I know all is well in those aforementioned categories (How did you like the use of my big word? Pop's becoming a real Shakespeare in his old age!)

I'm also proud of the moments we have shared. I mean, how many daughters have ever asked for power tools in their wedding registry? The thing about it was you not only asked for and got them; you became damn good at using all of them. While I'm writing this letter, I can imagine you using the table saw, the power router, and that industrial size drill to make a piece of furniture for one, if not all, of the wonderful grandchildren you have given me.

The memories just flood my mind. The way you cried over that military veteran we stopped to help along the side of the road. How beautiful you looked on your sixteenth birthday while I took you on a date and gave you your first Esmeraldas. The time you remodeled the interior of that '78 Camaro, the time I came home from a date at 1 a.m., and you were cleaning the house because you had to be at work early the next morning.

In fact, my memories are only superseded (another big word!) by your personal accomplishments. Besides being a great wife and mother, you're one hell of a computer instructor: 700 kids is a lot of students to teach. The incredible things you sew and crochet, and, man those delicious pumpkin pecan pies, they're the greatest thing since sliced bread.

As you know, Pop's had his share of health problems. But I have and will always figure out a way–with God's help–to work around life's little roadblocks.

Always remember, the Lord's not going to toss anything your way that you can't handle.

Love always and always,
Pop

✓ To My Grandkids

Dear Savannah, Summer, Sierra and Serena,

As you read this book, you may wonder why Grandpa decided to say so much. God knows I've never been known as a chatterbox!

I could tell you that somebody insisted I help him write this book, but that would be a lie. I wrote this book so you would get to know me even better than you do. There are things said here I've never shared with you. In fact, there are things said here I've never shared with anyone.

By now, you realize that Papa Cado had endured more pain and suffering than most. But that's okay, really. I'm not asking anybody to feel sorry for me because I've also had more blessings than most. The four of you are a living testament to that reality.

The trick is never to let the negatives outweigh the positives. I realize there a few stories in this book that may seem far-fetched, but they did happen. And, they are part of what made your Papa who he is.

Most of all, this book is my way of sharing my values with you. Values I learned from my mother and father and hopefully passed on to your mom. As you get older, I hope that you reflect on your spiritual roots. I also pray you will choose to live by them. And, one day, when you have children of your own, you will pass those values on to them.

In that way, our family will have a clear path to heaven, so that one day we can all be together again.

Love,
Papa

✓ To Teresa

Dear Long Lost Daughter,

Life certainly has a funny way of happening.

I've thought of you many times over the years. In fact, about eight years ago I explained what had happened to your sister Mindy and my wife, Susan.

They knew from the tone in my voice, finding you would close an important chapter in my life. Anyway, we did our best but found nothing.

So, when your letter arrived, I was stunned. It's hard to put in words my emotions at that moment, but they covered the gamut from love to embarrassment. Like everybody, I've made some stupid decisions in my life, but abandoning you was probably at the top of the deck.

I also wanted to mention something important. When we met in my hospital room for the first time, I asked if you had a happy life. Remember? Even though you quickly responded, "yes," there was something in the tone of your voice that said otherwise.

As we've gotten to know each other a bit, I've learned a lot. Having a 10-year old sister that was murdered by a neighbor in your house ran chills through my spine. And, learning you struggled for identity in a family of naturally-born children must have had its difficulties. But, you may have heard me say, God gives everybody little tests, but he never gives you more than you can handle. Plus, you're a Mercado. We never have and never will go down without a fight.

As you can plainly see, I'm not in the best of health. Without sounding maudlin, I will probably leave you again. But, it's different this time. You and have reconnected. So, when we meet again upstairs, our souls will immediately recognize each other. I think that will be God's signal that we passed all of his little tests with flying colors.

Till forever,
Your Loving Father

✓ To Paul

Dear Paul,

Needless to say, I've had some great doctors these past 30 years, but you are hands-down the best. No matter how crappy I feel when we go in that Cath Lab, I know I'm going to come out feeling a lot better.

I know you are one of the busiest and most respected cardiologists in the world. So I especially appreciate that little extra effort I know you put into my every visit, every review of my latest X-Rays, every piece of advice you give me as a patient.

But what blows me away is that fact that you always have time for me as a person. During our years together I can only say I am honored by the decencies you have extended to me as a slightly-used and quite inarticulate human being. It means so much to me, Susan, and my whole family.

They know you are my guardian angel. God bless and keep you well for another hundred years!

Your biggest fan,
Arthur

P.S. With a little luck, I can be your patient again, on my second time around!

✔ To Matt

My Crazy Matt,

I'm still trying to figure out why you picked me to write a book about!

When you first brought up the subject, I figured you must have been smoking some real good stuff. Then as you generously donated your time, and the memories began to flood my mind, I figured, what the hell, at least it could be a way for the family to remember their Papa Cado.

Now, I don't want to burst your bubble, but to think my personal drivel will be interesting to anybody but my family is beyond far-fetched. But I have my dreams, so who am I to say you shouldn't have yours?

All I know is that working with you these past months has meant a lot. For a guy who hardly spoke, now I can't shut up. When I pull into a gas station, I'm telling damn stories to perfect strangers. It's completely nuts!

You've also made me realize how much I have to live for despite my little medical hiccups.

In some ways, working on the book has re-energized my heart and soul. But most importantly, I feel I have made a new friend. A friend who will forever be a part of my family.

Love and laughs,
Your Brother Arthur

✓ To Diane

Dear Diane,

I have thought of you often these past 50 years. I know I hurt you deeply by abandoning you and our baby when you needed me most. For that, I am truly sorry.
I know you loved me and I loved you. I never meant to hurt you.

I'm so glad our daughter Teresa made the extraordinary effort to find her biological parents. It is hard to imagine that fifty years have passed in the blink of an eye. I am so glad you found a good man, have two sons, another daughter, and three grandchildren, and that life has treated you kindly, I hope. You deserve all that and more.

As you noticed at our tearful reunion in my hospital room, I'm a bit under the weather. God has given me a bunch of little tests. But each has made me stronger in the belief that he never gives you more than you can handle.

My friend Matt, who made this book possible, tells me that I will be an inspiration to those long after I'm gone. I don't know about that. All I know is you should greet each day with a smile, and live it to the fullest because you never know when the curtain will fall.

I've also made it my business to learn something new each day. The world is a wonderful place.

When you walked back into my life, I could truly say I am the luckiest man in the world. I've loved two women with all my heart. To see you and Susan stand side by side smiling at me filled my heart with an inner peace impossible to describe in words.

Given the current state of my health, I will most likely leave here before both of you. So God bless and goodbye, until we meet in another place at another time.

With love, respect and fond memories,
Arthur

✔ To Susan

Dear Love of My Life,

You have made me the happiest man in the world these past 19 years. I'm not sure I've ever told you that directly. More than that, you have become my reason to live. While we know I pride myself on being emotionally tough, the fact is you are the true rock in our family.

I have watched you hold each of our grandchildren at birth; I've watched those children become your children. It warms my heart every time those pictures flash in my mind.

You are the sun when it rains. The full moon when darkness descends. But, most of all you are "my moment of truth." You have made me understand the purpose of my life. And I hope in some small way what I have written will inspire others to find their own truth. Because, without truth, one cannot truly love himself or another.

My wishes are modest and my promises many. I wish I had met you earlier, so our time here would have been longer. I wish you had met Mom and Pop. They would have loved you. And Pop would have asked you why did you fall for a chump like me.

I wish you had been there to help guide Mindy. I did the best I know how. You would have made it better. I wish I had all the money in the world to give you everything you have ever wanted. You deserve that and more. I wish my health had not taken us on so many emotional roller coaster rides.

I promise to love you forever. And, I know one day we will be together forever.

I promise to take each day one at a time. I promise to be the very best husband, friend, and lover I can be. I promise never to whine or complain about anything.

Most importantly, I want no tears, no sadness at my discomforts, just your beautiful smile when I wake each day and when I fall asleep at night.

Love now and forever,
Arthur

Part Six

Letters to Arthur

✓ To Arthur Extraordinaire

Dear Arthur,

It was so nice of Matt to ask me to put down my thoughts about you. I'm proud and honored to do so.

You are quite simply one of the most extraordinary patients I have ever had, and, as you know, I've been doing this cardiologist thing for a long time.

You are a poster child for "the will to live with dignity and grace."

I'm not sure you realize that your incredible persistence, your sense of humor, your warm smile and positive attitude has reached legend status not only in the Cath Lab but around the halls of Scripps Green Hospital. My hope is that one day the inspiring story of your life and your grace under fire will touch people all over the world.

What has always impressed me is your care and concern for my staff and your patients, no matter what level of discomfort you might be experiencing.

As I've said to you on more than one occasion, I see no reason why we cannot continue to give you a long-lasting quality of life.

Keep up the good work. Never change. I'm confident your approach to healing will inspire many others to stay the course.

Your cardiologist and head cheerleader,
Paul

✔ To My Poppy

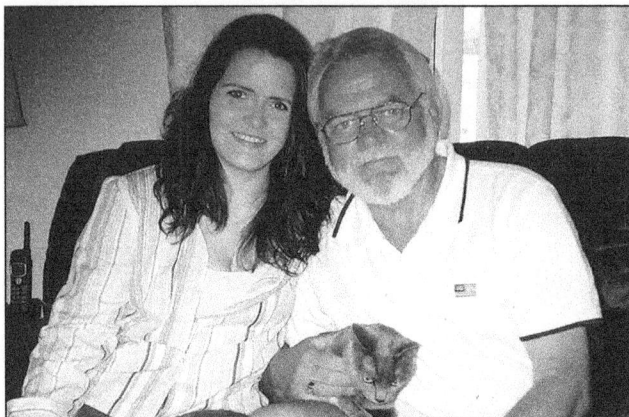

Dear Poppy,

I'm not your typical woman because I wasn't raised by a typical Pop.

From the get-go, I've always believed you were, and still are, the greatest Pop on earth! You taught me I could be anything I wanted to be, but you also taught me to have respect for tradition and always to carry myself as a lady. One day I could dress like a lady and carry a purse, and the next day catch the biggest fish. It was not only okay; you encouraged it. You taught me balance. And you can sleep easy because I'm teaching your granddaughters the same values. Rest assured, they all believe they can be anything they want to be.

You also taught me to savor our memories together. Do you remember holding me in your arms on the back porch in a rocking chair as we listened to John Denver? I'm guessing I was no more than two. And, how many kids can say they helped their Pop skin a deer at the age of three? Went fishing for trout or frog gigging before they ever went to school? Dressed up like a woman on her sixteenth birthday and received the most beautiful emerald ring in the whole world?

Pop, besides being my teacher and moral compass, you were, and still are, my best friend. We were all we had, and we had a great time. My only regret is we do not see more of each other since you remain a Southern Californian, and we make our home in Utah.

You know I also loved Grandma like crazy, the red-headed spitfire from Alabama. But, did I ever mention, the primary reason I changed the color of my hair from blond to auburn was to honor her fiery spirit?

I've got to get going now. The kids need to get to school, and then I've got to teach my computer class. But, I want you to know, I'll always love you. I remember how you used to say, if you love somebody, tell them because you may not be able to do so the next time.

You'll also be in my thoughts next Tuesday. I know you'll come through the stent procedure just fine. You always do. Besides, I'm not sure God and his buddies are ready for your sense of humor just yet!

Your proud, loving daughter,
Mindy Pooh

✔ To My Father

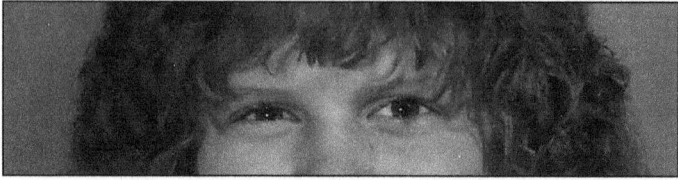

Dear Dad,

I'm so happy on found you after 50 years. You will never know how complete you've made my life. I only regret I didn't try to find you sooner.

I hope you enjoyed my picture album. I prepared it especially for y

As you know from our short time together, life has been hard as an adopted child that didn't quite fit in a family of five *regular* children. You will never know how lonely it feels to be the least important part of a family.

When I walked in that hospital for the first time, and you hugged me and said, "just like I thought, you are so beautiful," you made me feel like the most important person in the world.

I've had the good fortune of meeting my real Mom, Diane, and spending time with your wife Susan, my half-sister Mindy—who is a beautiful young lady by the way—and your friend Matt. His book has provided me a great primer on all things that have happened in your extraordinary life.

Clearly, you are a survivor like me. Or rather, I should say thanks to your DNA inside me; I have been a survivor like you.

More importantly, your life, and the obstacles you have overcome make you an inspiration to so many lives.

I will tell my children what I've learned about you, and how I feel towards you. They will be proud of their real grandfather.

The picture I have chosen to use with this letter may seem a bit strange, but think about it: my eyes are your eyes.

Love for all eternity,
Teresa

✔ To My First Love

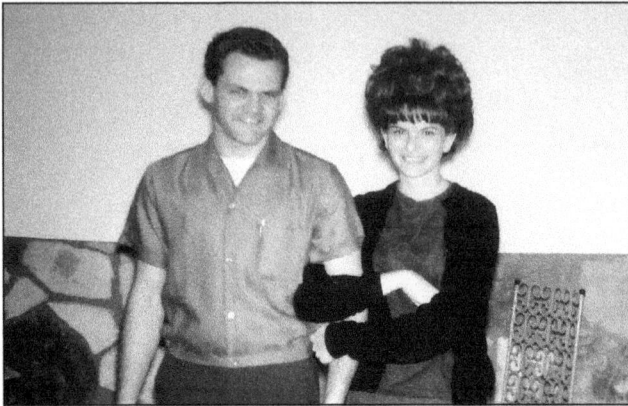

Dearest Art,

I guess, we are living proof that sometimes things don't turn out as you've imagined or could have hoped for.

Over the years I've regretted putting our baby up for adoption, and for the many things we should have talked about. But I was 20 and things were moving so fast, and I was so confused about so many things about us. Will also regret that I did not call you myself, after the party, to find out what went wrong that night.

I am so glad, our daughter Teresa persisted in finding us, when you, nor I could find her. It's hard to believe when Teresa and I walked into your hospital room, 50 years had passed. I just wanted to hug you, and feel your arms around me one last time.

I am happy that you met and married Susan, she's a wonderful person and glad she was there to take care of you. But, I would be less than honest if I didn't say I have missed you, missed your warmth, missed your strength, missed your love, and, yes, your unique sense of humor that made me laugh so many times. I would have liked to have been the one to take care of you when all your troubles began.

After reading an earlier edition of *Papa Cado* and talking to Susan, I learned so many things we have in common, that I didn't know about when we dated so long ago, up to the present time, our likes are so many!

For some reason, fate was not on our side. Sadly, we never had a chance to see where our love for each other could have taken us.

Perhaps we'll meet again in another time in another place?

Love always and forever...until that next time around,
Diane

✓ To the Man of My Forever Dreams

Dearest Husband,

The first time we met, I thought you were a nice guy. By the second time we met, I knew I wanted to spend the rest of my life with you. But I never imagined in my wildest dreams the ride we'd have together. And I wouldn't change a thing.

While we've had to deal with a few bad breaks, I am amazed every day how you maintain that wonderful sense of humor. How it gives you and me the strength to handle anything that God passes our way. Don't ever stop laughing.

Being around you this past decade has brought me great comfort; I hope my presence in your life has done the same for you. We have been blessed with the ability to cheer each other up. You've made me feel special from the first day we met. No man has ever done that for me, all the time, every day. I cherish every one of those miniature Swarovski crystal flowers, birds, and animals that you have given me. They are so thoughtful; don't ever stop. As you say about helping others, I only wish I could do more for you. You have done more for me than you could ever imagine

I know you laugh at the way I hover over you now and then, like one part wife, one part mother. But it is out of love and affection. I also get a kick out of the way you pout when I say you shouldn't be eating this or that. Although I will admit, you act less and less like a little boy with each passing year. By the time you're 80 or 85, I guess you'll be all grown up!

By the way, the other day I was telling your friend Matt about some of the changes I've seen in our two decades together. I told him I had watched you mellow, that the Mercado edge was fast dissipating. He laughed and said, "You must be talking about another Arthur Mercado."

I want to make sure you understand something, clearly and always. Your "little" health problems are not a burden. I will always be by your side. Now and forever.

I know Mindy describes you as the best Pop in the whole world. I also want you to know you are also the best husband in the whole world and my very best friend.

Love always and always,
Susan

✔ To My Hero, My Role Model

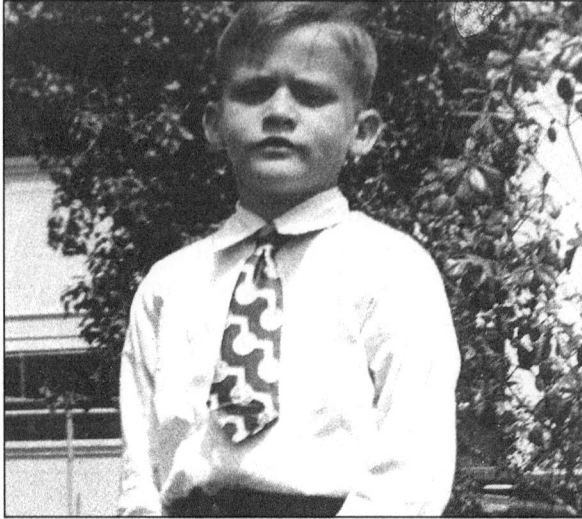

Dear Arthur,

I wanted to thank you for giving me the extraordinary privilege of allowing me to become part of your life.

When we began our journey to chronicle your life, my hope and dream was that the love and laughter you carries into each day would inspire others to think and act likewise. And in some small way make the world a better place for all of us.

I never imagined our journey would change my life forever. I do not delude myself that I am a better man, but I'm certainly a different man because a part of you is now a part of me.

Our bond, our friendship is now enrolled in the book of eternity. You have been a forever Christmas present come early.

The other day I was sitting in my family room watching that wonderful movie, *A League of Their Own*. You know the one where a group of young ladies do something that's never been done—create a women's baseball league. They had a moment that would last forever. Then, many years later revisited that moment at a women's baseball museum built in their honor. It so much reminded me of our experience together. We've had our moment, and this book will be our museum. A place where you, me, our families and our families' families can revisit again and again.

I've thought long and hard about how to close my letter to you. And, I always return to the same place. The haunting lyrics of the theme song to that movie..."Now and Forever."

Given our experience together, the lyrics took on a new meaning. I thought it only appropriate to make them my final thought to you. By the way, if this book were a CD, I would have copied the song five times, just as you do!

Forever in your debt,
Crazy Matt

...We had a moment
Just one moment
That will last beyond a dream,
beyond a lifetime
We are the lucky ones
Some people never get to do
All we got to do
Now and forever
I will always think of you
Now and forever
I will always be with you...

© Carole King

Part Seven

Lessons Learned

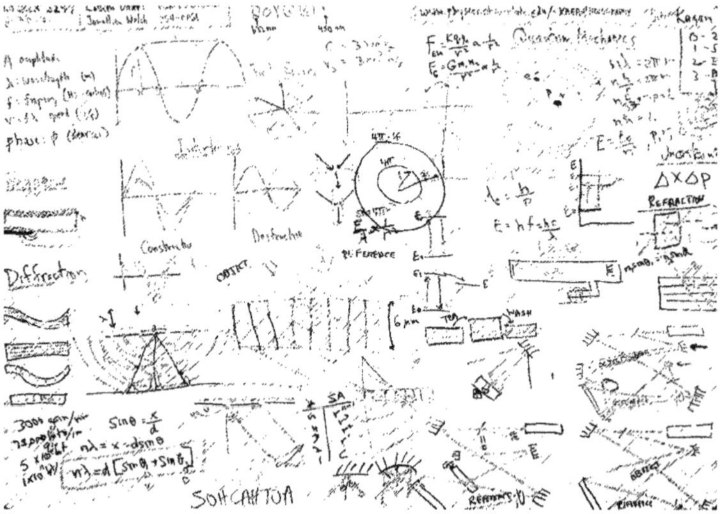

1. Adversity

*Arthur exits Cath Lab at Scripps Hospital after procedure number 46
or 47, he can't remember exactly.*

"Feeling sorry for yourself doesn't make anything better.
Just do something."

"If you ever wonder why one person (you) has to deal
with so much negative stuff, just look around. There's
always some- body dragging with a bigger bag."

"You should absolutely, positively feel very, very guilty
about whining so much."

"Determination can overcome a hell of a lot of obstacles."

"Always ask, "How am I doing today'?" Then move to
the side as the depressing, negative crap flows down the
hill!"

"When a man can handle anything that comes his way
without complaining, he officially becomes a man."

"In life, crap always happens, but there's no manual about
how to deal with it."

"Never lose faith, no matter how the odds seem stacked."

"Things always go on as they should...eventually."

"The best was to deal with a bad hand is to find another deck of cards or change blackjack tables."

2. Common Sense

Arthur tinkers with his metal detector before hitting the beaches of Southern California.

"If you spot a rattlesnake and he's not bothering you, leave the damn thing alone."

"Feeling sorry for yourself is more trouble than a blowout on a slippery, wet road."

"I believe everybody has some a secret they've never told anybody. I just don't know if that's good or bad."

"Life's a lot like a barrel of snakes. Some people learn to keep away from trouble the first time out. Fools need to make the same mistake a few more times before they get religion."

"A grown man should never lose his sense of humor because laughter makes everything right with the world."

"Sometimes you do things that have no real meaning, but you spend forever trying to figure out what nothing means."

"If your child ever asks for a little white headed pet monkey, adamantly refuse and offer to buy them a baby tiger cub instead."

"Having good memories is the next best thing to doing what you want to do, but can't."

"The best time to go metal-detecting on the beach is after a rain storm or a high tide because good stuff gets buried inches below the sand line."

"I learned there are no free rides in life; everybody has responsibilities."

"Once you make a commitment to something, there's no backpedaling."

"Only-if- I-had guilt can last a lifetime, so be certain it really was your fault."

3. Death

Renowned cardiologist Paul Tierstein (l) and his team, who have kept Arthur alive through some 50 plus procedures, mug for the camera with another Tierstein patient, Mother Teresa.

"Don't ask for second opinions when you're dying."

"Never lose faith, no matter how much the doctors tell you the odds are stacked against you."

"Let people know you've been here. Leave a legacy, not by what you say, or you accomplish in materials terms, but by your actions."

"Knowing somebody that died and came back to life makes you a lot friendlier."

"There are no medals awarded to dead people who died of stupidity."

"All the stuff we hold so important really isn't. If you don't believe me, ask yourself, if this was your last day, how important would it be?"

"The more out-of-body experiences you have, the harder it is to rejoin the living. One should be enough for everybody."

"Talking to someone you love in a moment of crisis makes everything right with the world."

"If the time comes when that there is no hope, make sure somebody is authorized to disconnect you; it avoids undue suffering for all concerned."

"You don't win any prizes for saving a doctor's time by waiting until you are absolutely, positively certain you are dying before you ask for help."

4. Fear

A self-confident (and younger) Arthur teases an angry copperhead snake dangling on the end of a tree branch in the desert.

"It's okay to be afraid. You just don't let it stop you from what you need to do."

"Always strive to make lemonade out of life's lemons."

"God is not in the business of giving a man more than he can handle. So, if you don't figure out how to work around it, the fault lies with you, not Him."

"No point in fearing death. You'll miss the party upstairs."

"The purpose of life is to avoid being lonely."

"Fear Not. If something sounds stupid, it probably is stupid."

5. Food

Arthur always preferred his rainbow trout fresh and natural. No Costco's or Walmart's for him

"Non-fat dressings don't work."

"Nothing like a good wholesome meal of black beans and thick gravy and a big slice of cherry pie."

"In life, you've got to drink the froth to get the beer."

"Being a male chef like James Beard isn't homo."

"When the doctor says you need a low-fat, low-salt diet, ask him if he's ever tried it."

"Roasting pecans in a leaf patch are delicious, but the random sparks can start a fire. I'm just not sure which generally happens first."

"Eating right usually doesn't taste good, and I'm not sure it helps you live any longer."

"Roasted rattlesnakes with a little ground pepper make great campfire snacks."

6. Gambling

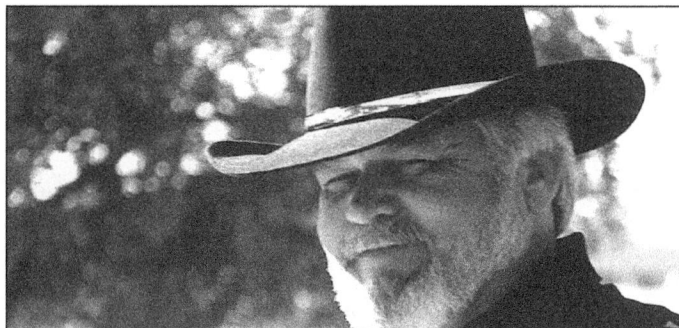

Arthur dons his gambling gear and heads to the blackjack tables at the Gold Nugget in Las Vegas.

"Gambling is a lot like playing golf. You may have a dreadful round, but you also remember the good holes, which keeps you coming back for more."

"When you're on a gambling hot streak, take all the money off the table and go have a lobster dinner. You've earned it."

"If you're going to try to win big by bluffing, you better have a solid backup plan, just in case."

"There are no DUI's when you gambling. Drinking makes you forget you're a loser."

"What's worse? Losing a ton at the blackjack table or dating a woman for all the wrong reasons."

"Ever try borrowing a $100 from a friend who claims they just had a big night at the crap tables?"

7. Laughter

Arthur's been close to death so many times, he feels a good laugh with friends is better medicine than another procedure at the hospital.

"If a flip phone is good enough for Warren Buffet, it's good enough for me."

"Not taking yourself too seriously will get you through life's tough moments."

"Laughing is a lot smarter than crawling into a corner and letting the world beat the crap out of you."

"If you want to complain about the hand you've been dealt, play solitaire. That way nobody has to listen to you moan and groan."

"If your pet goldfish dies, give him or her underwater CPR. Miracles do happen."

"Amuse yourself. It's not important if people don't find your jokes funny."

"Keep telling yourself, "I've still got it," even if you can remember what "it" is."

"Never underestimate the coolness of a cool nerd."

8. Love

Arthur and the love of his life, Susan, on their wedding days, some twenty years ago. (She had no idea what she was getting herself into.)

"If you fall in love with somebody, brace yourself for that moment of separation. It will last a long time."

"Never enter a heavy relationship unless you really love that someone. Then never stop telling them you love them."

"If you love somebody without reservation, it's not going to hurt anyone if you admit it sooner rather than later."

"When you fall in love make sure they love you back. If they don't, save time and aggravation: get on with your life."

"Being loved unconditionally is the greatest feeling in the world."

"Exposing the people you love to your softer side transmits strength, not vulnerability."
"If you decide to fall in love, make sure she knows."

"The size of your heart has nothing to do with the size of your body."

"Talking to someone you love in a moment of crisis makes everything right with the world."

"The right woman completes your life. But the wrong women...."

9. Medicine

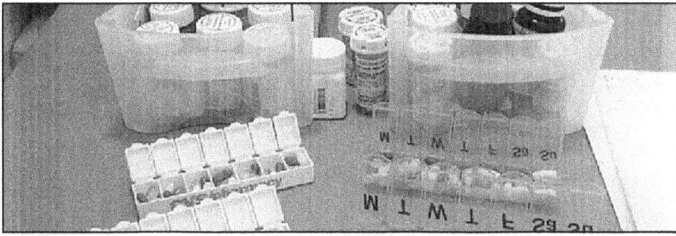

In Arthur's case, 24 plus prescriptions a day doesn't seem to keep the doctor's away.

"Expect a little post-round discomfort when you play 18 holes of golf with a torn rotator cuff and a few fresh stents in your arteries."

"If you experience a lull between stent procedures, make hay while the sun shines."

"There is no such thing as a routine' invasive surgery."

"Getting stents inserted is a lot like being married. Assume pain, even though you're not sure when and how it will be delivered."

"Having a stent inserted in one of your arteries is a lot like baking cupcakes. If the blood flows smoothly through the stent, you're done. Just like when the toothpick cleanly slides out of the cupcake."

"If poor health makes you a frequent guest at emergency rooms and Cath Labs, go to the same ones, so they get to know your lifestyle preferences (e.g., heated blankets, head phones and gurneys located in quiet corners, etc)."

"If you simply "must" have a stent procedure, surround yourself with beautiful nurses. It's a lot more fun!"

10. Money

A young Arthur and his Pop liked to spend their money refurbishing old cars.

"The beaches of Southern California have been over "metal detected because people would rather surf than work.""

"Integrity is never for sale."

"When searching for wealth on the beach with a metal detector only use a four-inch ice pick when the beach is deserted otherwise, beachgoers get all upset and yell for the police."

"Money is lot women; you can't live with 'em and you can't live without 'em."

"Money was never meant for showing off."

"Figure out what somebody wants before you make your final offer. It may not be money."

"Money is the root cause of all happiness, after love."

"Once you build a revolving balance on a credit card, you'll never pay it off."

11. Nightmares

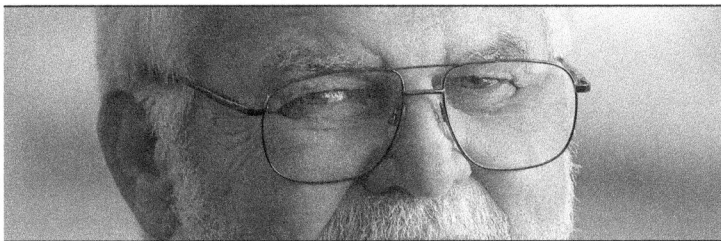

While nightmares created by drug interactions are scary to many, Arthur embraces them as conversation starters.

"Doctors prescribe drugs like popcorn because they know pharmaceutical interactions stimulate your mind's creative juices."

"Parkinson nightmares are very graphic. They are a lot like being married to the wrong women."

"Recurring nightmares can make great YouTube videos if you know how to use those fancy computer apps."

"Don't waste a dollar on psychiatrists, nightmares were designed to make no sense."

"Nightmares make for a great discussion at barber shops that still have that pole going around."

"People like happy people. Even sad people like happy people. So, if don't want friends, start describing your weird, depress- ing nightmares."

12. Parkinson's

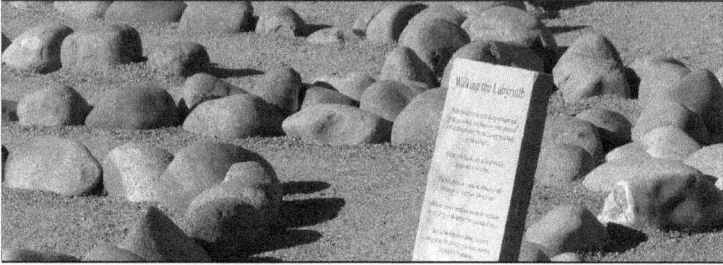

Arthur's formula to stave off his decade long battle with Parkinson's?
Grit+determination+humility+laughter. (Lots of it).

"Congratulations, if you've got Parkinson's. Now you can enjoy donuts whenever you want, so long as they're not filled with jelly, custard or cream."

"Gotta remember, Doctors are human, they can only do so much, after that it up to you to keep it going."

"One of the best things about Parkinson's is the further it progresses the less you remember that you forgot something."

"Give yourself credit; your mind is a lot stronger than you think."

"Parkinson's shortens idle phone chatter with boring people." "Parkinson's eliminates the need for worthless text messages.

"Parkinson's help you eat more of what you like without gaining weight."

"People want to feel sorry for you, so you never have to do things you don't want to do."

"Because you speak slower with Parkinson's, people think you sound smarter than you are."

"Parkinson's is like a good-field, no-hit baseball player. You may have a season or two that exceeds expectations, but eventually, your weak bat brings you back to reality."

13. Reality

Arthur's heart-healthy support group. Arthur and emotional guru Dr. Ozzie Gontag (bottom). Friends Keith, Don, Kris, and Matt (top).

"Make sure you cultivate the left side of your brain because a little imagination can sure go a long way."

"Everybody makes stupid decisions as they pass through life. But you better figure out how to fix them, otherwise you'll die one unhappy dude."

"Sometimes, cool just comes to those who wait."

"When real opportunity knocks, don't be a grumpy old pig. Open the damn door and invite him in."

"If it looks like a duck, acts like a duck, waddles like a duck, quacks like a duck, and smells like a duck, it's a duck. Some people just smell the duck shit sooner than others."

"A little imagination and a lot of hard work can deliver unimagined good fortune. (It also might not, so lighten up.)"

"If what you're contemplating seems stupid, don't do it because it probably is stupid."

"If somebody suggests your idea is stupid then do it because they are probably stupid."

"It's perfectly normal to want to do more with your life, but it's depressing abnormal to obsess about what you haven't achieved."

"Cool is what cool sees."

"Life's a lot like a barrel of snakes. Some people learn to keep away from trouble the first time out. Others need to make the same mistake a few more times before they back away."

14. Sensitivity

Susan's recent birthday gift represents the sum of Arthur the man: heart of a Lion and gentle as a Lamb.

"Animals are living creatures that can teach you how to be a more sensitive, caring person than you've ever imagined."

"Generosity and compassion for other people get returned ten-fold."

"If more parents and their children showed mutual respect, the need to take stern disciplinary actions would be few and far between."

"There is a fine line between a demeaning handout and an act of loving generosity."

"When you don't know what to say, just say thank you."

"Always be respectful of others, even if you disagree. But stand your ground. Otherwise, you'll get your ass trampled in the stampede."

"Always be respectful of others. But, if they disrespect you or your family, act first, think about it second."

"Never lose your self-confidence, it's what makes a man a man."

"No matter how little or how much God gives you, make sure you share."

15. Self Defense

Arthur loved to hunt (again when younger). His favorite gun was a classic Ithaca, which he bought from an old man in the dessert.

"Be kind and gentle with people, unless they give you crap. Then be prepared to kick their ass!"

"When you get into a fight, never underestimate the power of your opponent, no matter how small they may appear."

"It's okay for a family to fight, but when somebody challenges your family, it's time to close ranks."

Because you can't reach out and touch something, does that mean it doesn't exist?"

"When does myth become a reality, if ever?"

"Once you make a commitment to something, there's no back peddling, unless you're a mealy mouth wimp."

"Kicking the crap out of a bunch of helpless golf balls is an emotionally gratifying experience."

16. Women

Arthur poses with the first love of his life, high-school sweetheart Diane in 1963. He remembered her beehive hairdo 53 years later.

"No matter how lonely you feel, be wary of well-meaning friends offering companionship with the 'perfect' blind date. It's usually they who are blind."

"Relationships are a lot like gambling. When you're on a hot streak with the opposite sex, take your winnings off the table and play with house money."

"All the beer in the world with all the friends in the world, may not be as rewarding as an evening with the most willing girl in the world."

"The ultimate pickup line: You're like a bubble gum sandwich. I want to chew you up."

"Coolness always greases cupid's arrows. But recognize the space between cool and arrogant is extremely narrow."

"If she flat out rejects your advances, don't sweat it. Rejection is a part of life, like peanut butter and jelly and croutons and Caesar salad."

"Firing a hunting rifle without knowing exactly what to expect is a lot like getting drunk and waking up married to the wrong woman."

"My relationships with women have taught me there is a time to say your piece and a time to keep your mouth shut."

"Don't cross a woman unless you want hell to pay!"

References

The Heart Speaks. Erminia Guarneri, M.D., FACC.
Touchstone Books, Simon & Schuster, 2011.

Visible Darkness. William Styron.
Vintage Books, Random House, 1992.

Growing Up Brave. Donna B. Pincus, Ph.D.
Hachette Books, Little, Brown and Company, 2012.

Modern Practices in Radiation Treatments.
Edited by Gopishankar Natanasabapathi.
intechopen.com Publishing, 2012.

Migraine and Headache. Alexander Mauskop.
Oxford American Pain Library, 2009.

Outsmarting Anger. Joseph Strand, M.D.
Harvard Health Publications, Harvard Medical School.

Coronary Artery Bypasses. Russell T. Hammond.
Nova Science Publishers, 2009.

Treating Gambling Problems. William A. Howatt.
John Wiley & Sons, 2007.

Stroke Rehabilitation. Glen Gillen, Ed.D.
Mosby Books, Elsevier Publishing, 2011.

Out of Body Experiences. Robert Peterson.
Hampton Roads Publishing, 1997.

Heart Disease Treatment with Angioplasty and Stents.
Web MD. www.webmd.com, 2013.

Angina, John P. Cunha, D.O., FACOEP.
www.onhealth.com, 2013.

Nitroglycerin and Other Nitrates. Health Sciences Library.
Upstate Medical University, 2013. library.upstate.edu

Stockley's Drug Interactions, 11th Edition. Edited by Clair L.
Preston. Pharmaceutical Press, 2016.

The Power of Self Help Groups.
www.allaboutcounseling.com, 2013.

The Psychology of C. G. Jung.
http://www.simplypsychology.org/carl-jung.html

On the Nature of the Psyche. C.G. Jung. London: Ark
Paperbacks, 1947.

Wit and its Relation to the Unconscious. Sigmund Freud.
Moffat, Yard & Co, 1917.

The Therapeutic Value of Laughter as Medicine.
http://europepmc.org/abstract/med/21280463

The Wisdom of Carl Jung, Edward Hoffman, Citadel Press,
2003.

The Study of the Effects of Humor on Perceived Pain and Effect.
Adams & McGuire, Haworth Press, 1986.

Parkinson's Sleep Disturbances. http://
pdcenter.neurology.ucsf.edu/patients-guide/sleep-and-
parkinsons-disease

Parkinson's Movement Disorders. John l. Campbell M.D. et al.
Movement Disorder Society. http://
onlinelibrary.wiley.com/doi/10.1002/mds.21922/full2008

www.ingramcontent.com/pod-product-compliance
Lightning Source LLC
Chambersburg PA
CBHW031236090426
42742CB00007B/219